OECD Economic Surveys:
Spain
2012

OECD

BETTER POLICIES FOR BETTER LIVES

This document and any map included herein are without prejudice to the status of or sovereignty over any territory, to the delimitation of international frontiers and boundaries and to the name of any territory, city or area.

Please cite this publication as:
OECD (2012), *OECD Economic Surveys: Spain 2012*, OECD Publishing.
http://dx.doi.org/10.1787/eco_surveys-esp-2012-en

ISBN 978-92-64-12832-3 (print)
ISBN 978-92-64-12833-0 (PDF)

Series: OECD Economic Surveys
ISSN 0376-6438 (print)
ISSN 1609-7513 (online)

OECD Economic Surveys: Spain
ISSN 1995-3364 (print)
ISSN 1999-0421 (online)

The statistical data for Israel are supplied by and under the responsibility of the relevant Israeli authorities. The use of such data by the OECD is without prejudice to the status of the Golan Heights, East Jerusalem and Israeli settlements in the West Bank under the terms of international law.

Photo credits: Cover © Westend61/Inmagine Ltd.

Corrigenda to OECD publications may be found on line at: *www.oecd.org/publishing/corrigenda*.

© OECD 2012

Table of contents

Boxes

Tables

Figures

This book has...

StatLinks

A service that delivers Excel® files from the printed page!

Look for the *StatLinks* at the bottom right-hand corner of the tables or graphs in this book. To download the matching Excel® spreadsheet, just type the link into your Internet browser, starting with the *http://dx.doi.org* prefix.

If you're reading the PDF e-book edition, and your PC is connected to the Internet, simply click on the link. You'll find *StatLinks* appearing in more OECD books.

This Survey is published on the responsibility of the Economic and Development Review Committee of the OECD, which is charged with the examination of the economic situation of member countries.

The economic situation and policies of Spain were reviewed by the Committee on 2 October 2012. The draft report was then revised in the light of the discussions and given final approval as the agreed report of the whole Committee on 24 October 2012.

The Secretariat's draft report was prepared for the Committee by Andrés Fuentes and Anita Wölfl under the supervision of Pierre Beynet. Statistical assistance was provided by Sylvie Foucher-Hantala.

The previous Survey of Spain was issued in December 2010.

BASIC STATISTICS OF SPAIN, 2011

The numbers in parentheses refer to the OECD average

LAND, PEOPLE AND ELECTORAL CYCLE

Population (1 000 000):	44.8		Population density per km²	88.7	(34.3)
Under 15 (%)	14.9	(18.4)	Life expectancy (years, 2010):	82.2	(79.7)
Over 65 (%)	17.6	(14.9)	Males	79.1	(76.9)
Foreign-born (%, 2010)	14.5		Females	85.3	(82.5)
Latest 5-year average growth (%)	0.3	(0.5)	Last general election:	November	2011

ECONOMY

GDP, current prices (billion USD)	1 479.6		Value added shares (%, 2010):		
GDP, current prices (billion, local currency)	1 063.4		Primary	2.5	(2.6)
Latest 5-year average real growth (%)	0.1	(0.8)	Industry incl. construction	27.0	(27.8)
GDP per capita, PPP (thousand USD)	33.1	(35.4)	Services	70.5	(69.5)

GENERAL GOVERNMENT

Expenditure (% of GDP)	44.1	(45.0)	Gross financial debt (% of GDP)	76.0	(99.2)
Revenue (% of GDP)	35.5	(36.8)	Net financial debt (% of GDP)	49.0	(59.8)

EXTERNAL ACCOUNTS

Exchange rate (EUR per USD)	0.719		Main exports (% of total merchandise exports, 2010):	
PPP exchange rate (USA = 1)	0.716			
Exports of goods and services (% of GDP)	30.3	(52.4)	Machinery and transport equipment	33.7
Imports of goods and services (% of GDP)	31.1	(49.3)	Manufactured goods	17.2
Current account balance (% of GDP)	-3.5	(-0.6)	Chemicals and related products	14.2
Net international investment position (% of GDP, 2010)	-92.5		Main imports (% of total merchandise imports, 2010):	
			Machinery and transport equipment	28.8
			Mineral fuels, lubricants and related materials	18.4
			Chemicals and related products	14.2

LABOUR MARKET, SKILLS AND INNOVATION

Employment rate (%) for 15-64 year olds:	57.7	(64.8)	Unemployment rate (%):	21.6	(7.9)
Males	63.2	(73.0)	Youth (%)	46.5	(16.2)
Females	52.0	(56.8)	Long-term unemployed (%)	9.0	(2.6)
Average worked hours per year	1 690	(1 776)	Tertiary educational attainment 25-64 year-olds (%, 2010)	31.0	(31.0)
Gross domestic expenditure on R&D (% of GDP, 2009)	1.4	(2.4)			

ENVIRONMENT

Total primary energy supply per capita (toe):	2.8	(4.3)	CO_2 emissions from fuel combustion per capita (tonnes, 2009)	6.2	(9.8)
Renewables (%)	11.4	(8.2)	Water abstractions per capita (dam³, 2009)	0.7	
Fine particulate matter concentration (urban, PM_{10}, µg/m³, 2008)	27.6	(22.0)	Municipal waste per capita (tonnes, 2010)	0.5	(0.5)

SOCIETY

Income inequality (Gini coefficient, %)	31.7	(31.4)	Education outcomes (PISA score, 2009):		
Relative poverty rate	20.6	(17.7)	Reading	481	(493)
Public and private spending (% of GDP):			Mathematics	483	(496)
Health care (2008)	9.0	(8.8)	Science	488	(501)
Pensions (2007)	8.6	(8.6)	Share of women in parliament (%, July 2012)	34.9	(24.4)
Education (2008)	3.1	(3.7)	Net official development assistance (% of GNI)	0.3	(0.4)

Better Life Index: *www.oecdbetterlifeindex.org/*

Note: An unweighted average of latest available data is used for the OECD average, calculated when data for at least 29 countries are available.
Source: OECD.STAT (*http://stats.oecd.org*); *OECD Economic Outlook Database.*

Executive summary

Spain is immersed in a prolonged recession. *The depressing impact on activity of private sector deleveraging and the need for sizeable fiscal consolidation following the bust of the domestic credit boom has been compounded by the euro area debt crisis and structural rigidities in the labour market, resulting in a steep increase in unemployment and a banking crisis. The prospect of an immediate recovery remains remote as deleveraging of the private sector still has a long way to go while the feedback loop between government finances and the banking sector remains strong, notwithstanding the loan of up to 100 billion euros from the euro area governments to recapitalise the banks. This feedback loop must be broken. Further structural reforms are needed to boost employment, notably among youth, and improve competitiveness, helping to reduce the current account deficit further. Given the major risks that have built up, decisive policy action on all these fronts is urgent if the situation is to be turned around.*

The financial crisis needs to be addressed quickly. *Progress has been made in the comprehensive recognition of losses, which is key for restoring confidence in the banking sector. The government has taken an important step by tightening the provisioning rules on the banks' real estate-related exposures. Rapid orderly resolution of non-viable banks and recapitalisation of viable banks with capital needs will be key, as planned in the Memorandum of Understanding with the European Union on a financial sector reform programme, which is a welcome framework. The impaired housing-related assets need to be transferred to the planned asset management company at prices which are sufficiently low to limit risks for public finances. Action needs to be taken to ensure that the substantial amounts of hybrid capital and debt buffers will share the burden of losses, especially when the holders of these instruments are institutional investors. Reform of bankruptcy procedures would help to shift resources from insolvent companies to productive use.*

Confidence in public finances needs to be restored. *To restore credibility, the government should aim at meeting its new headline deficit targets adopted in July 2012, unless GDP growth is far lower than expected, in which case the automatic stabilisers should be allowed to operate, at least partially. Reform of budgetary rules across all levels of government and recent consolidation measures mark substantial progress. The rules need to be strictly implemented, notably to improve regional government finances. They should be backed up with an independent fiscal council, as planned by the government, to assess budgetary policies at all levels of government. The consolidation measures needed to reach the deficit target in 2014 and the permanent budgetary measures needed to stabilise government debt should be spelled out. There is further scope for tax reform to contribute to budgetary consolidation and make the tax system more green-growth friendly. Further pension reform would improve long-term sustainability and improve incentives to move activity from the black to the formal economy.*

Addressing very high unemployment requires a broad range of reforms. *The unemployment rate in Spain has reached painfully high levels, in particular among young people with low levels of education. The 2012 labour market reform makes significant progress in addressing some key structural weaknesses of the labour market, notably as concerns employment protection and collective bargaining. If the reform does not prove effective, more steps could be taken to reduce labour market duality by moving towards a single contract. An option to improve the flexibility to adapt to economic conditions would be to abolish the legal extension of collective bargaining outcomes, or to replace it by an opt-in system. Quick action is also needed to improve the effectiveness of placement services. More job-search assistance and training must be provided, especially for the young unemployed, and active labour market programmes need to be targeted to the most vulnerable groups. Job-search requirements for receiving unemployment benefits need to be tightened. Action should also be taken to prevent youth from dropping out of education at a very early stage. Steps to better match skills with firms' demands can improve the school-to-work transition: the government is taking steps to reform vocational education, which is welcome.*

Key recommendations

Macroeconomic policies to stabilise the economy and buttress the banking sector

- Viable banks with capital needs should be recapitalised promptly and non-viable banks should be resolved in an orderly manner as soon as possible, as foreseen in the Memorandum of Understanding.

- Holders of subordinated debt and lower-ranked hybrid capital instruments should absorb losses of banks which are resolved or are restructured, as foreseen in the Memorandum of Understanding.

- The government should aim at meeting its new headline deficit targets, unless growth is far lower than expected, in which case the automatic stabilisers should be allowed to operate, at least partially.

- The consolidation measures needed to reach the deficit target in 2014 should be spelt out. Their regressive impact, if any, should be minimised, to foster the social consensus around consolidation needs.

- To improve the fiscal framework, establish a fiscal council with a strong mandate. Strictly implement control of regional government budget policies and the new requirements on the publication of regional government budget outcomes.

- Raise taxes on environmental externalities, including on transport fuels. Apply the standard VAT tax rate to more goods and services. Make increases in the taxation of real estate values permanent and reduce taxation of housing transactions.

Labour and product market policies to boost employment and growth

- Further reduce compensation for unjustified dismissal. If the reform does not prove to be effective, a single contract with initially low but gradually increasing severance payments would reduce the still large difference in dismissal costs between temporary and permanent contracts. This would help reduce duality effectively.

- An option to improve the flexibility to adapt to economic conditions is to abolish legal extension of higher level collective bargaining agreements or replace it by an opt-in system, where employers decide whether to be represented in sectoral wage bargaining.

- Extend access to training and job-search assistance for unemployed youth. Introduce comprehensive monitoring and benchmarking of placement services and ALMP implementation at regional level.

- Widen access to upper secondary education by narrowing criteria for grade advancement in lower secondary education to core competencies. Combine the school-based vocational education system and training contracts into one single scheme.

- Further reduce the costs and procedures necessary to create businesses and eliminate sector-specific entry barriers, including for professional services as well as rail and road transport.

- Entry barriers for large-surface retail outlets imposed by regional governments should be lowered, and shop opening hours should be liberalised in those regions where restrictions remain. Raise the national minimum limit on hours that regions have to apply when regulating shop opening hours.

Assessment and recommendations

The economy is suffering a protracted recession

The economy is undergoing a prolonged recession since the outbreak of the global crisis in late 2008. The bust of the housing boom and persistent domestic structural weaknesses, especially in the labour market, have been compounded by the European debt crisis. Deleveraging in the private sector has resulted in a contraction of domestic demand, adding to mass unemployment and generating high government deficits (Figure 1). The feedback loops between confidence in government solvency and banking sector health, which reflect in part the absence of appropriate euro area institutions (OECD 2011a, 2011b), have resulted in high risk spreads on interest rates for government debt (Figure 2). This in turn has raised funding costs for banks and has kept lending conditions tight.

Exceptional liquidity provision by the European Central Bank (ECB) has only provided a temporary relief. Private external funding has been increasingly withdrawn and ECB funding for the banks has filled the funding gap. As a result, the net negative position of the *Banco de España* (including the Target 2 balance) vis-à-vis the eurosystem has risen, mostly reflecting recourse of Spanish banks to ECB long-term funding, while foreign holdings of Spanish bank and government debt have diminished markedly. In the short term, there is a substantial risk that the economy, notably the banks, will remain cut off from external funding. This would deepen the recession, especially if measures taken at the European level prove ineffective in easing tensions in interbank and sovereign markets. However, the rapid introduction of common bank regulation and direct recapitalisation of banks with euro area funds may eventually diminish the negative feedback loops between bank financial positions and sovereign spreads. Launching the new unlimited bond-buying programme (OMT) in the context of an EFSF or ESM programme would also help to reduce spreads on sovereign debt.

Against this adverse backdrop, the immediate policy priority is to restore confidence in the banking sector by rapidly recapitalising viable banks with capital shortfalls, resolving orderly non-viable banks and isolating doubtful assets into a an asset management company as foreseen in the Memorandum of Understanding agreed between the Spanish and the European authorities in the context of the requested external financial assistance for the recapitalisation of financial institutions. Exiting the negative feedback loop will also require a credible medium-term strategy to return public finances to a sustainable path, as well as making bond holders contribute to bank recapitalisation and loss absorption in banks. The government has responded to these challenges with a wide-ranging programme, including substantial budgetary consolidation and the reinforcement of budgetary rules, as well as labour market and banking sector reforms. Based on these ambitious reforms and a Memorandum of Understanding agreed with the European Union, the government can use the loan of up to 100 billion euros (9½ per cent of GDP) granted by euro area governments to recapitalise Spanish banks. These reforms have the potential to generate significant

Figure 1. **Recent macroeconomic developments**

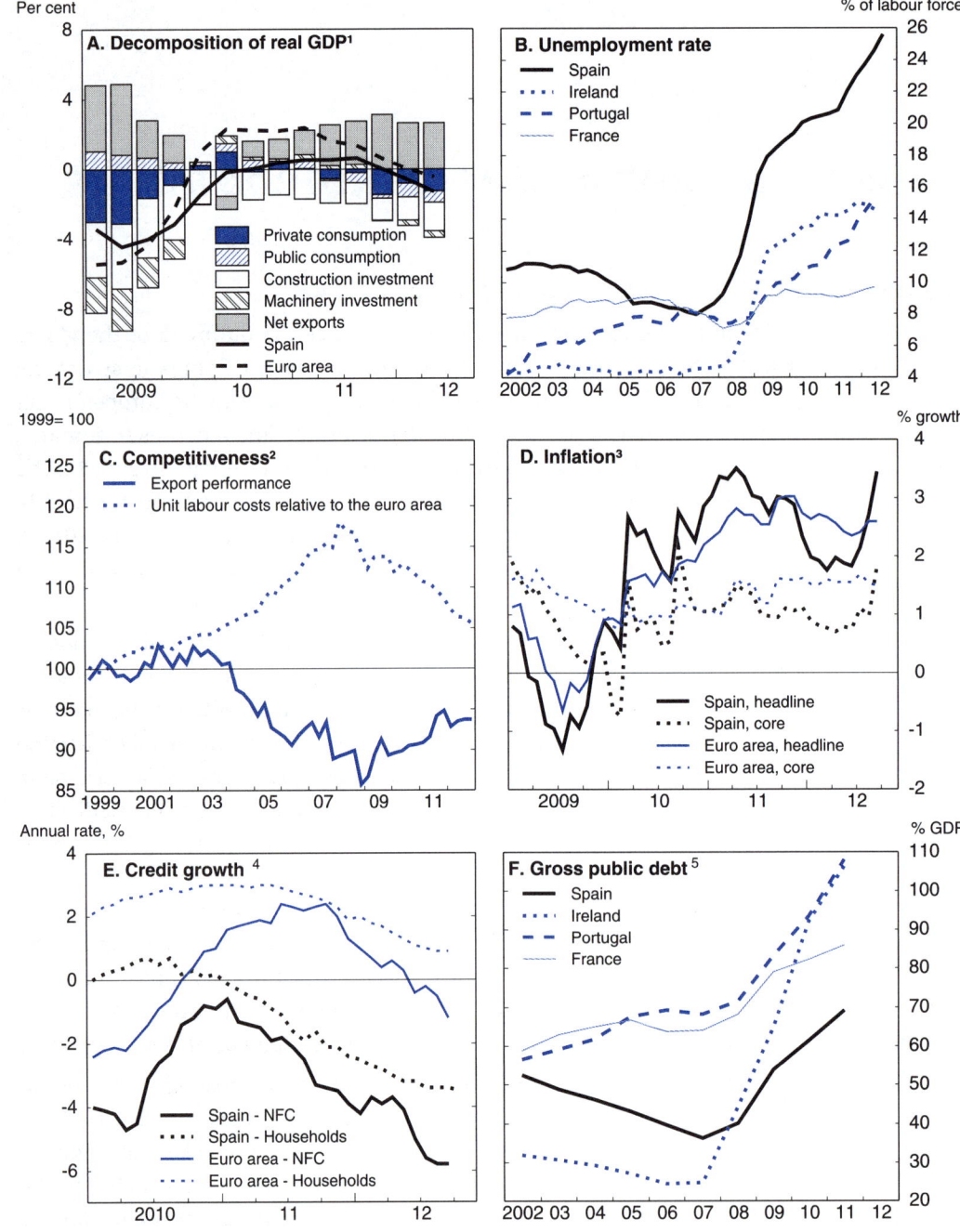

1. Contributions to growth, year-on-year. The lines represent real GDP growth.
2. Unit labour costs for total economy. Export performance is the ratio between export volumes and export markets for total goods and services.
3. Inflation is measured by the year-on-year change in the consumer price index. Core inflation excludes food and energy.
4. Loans adjusted for sales and securitisation. NFC: non-financial corporations. Households includes non-profit institutions serving households.
5. Maastricht definition.

Source: OECD (2012), *OECD Economic Outlook: Statistics and Projections* and *Main Economic Indicators Databases*, November; and ECB (2012), Statistical Data Warehouse, European Central Bank, November.

StatLink ᘛᓵ⅃ *http://dx.doi.org/10.1787/888932740195*

Figure 2. **Recent financial market developments**
Basis points

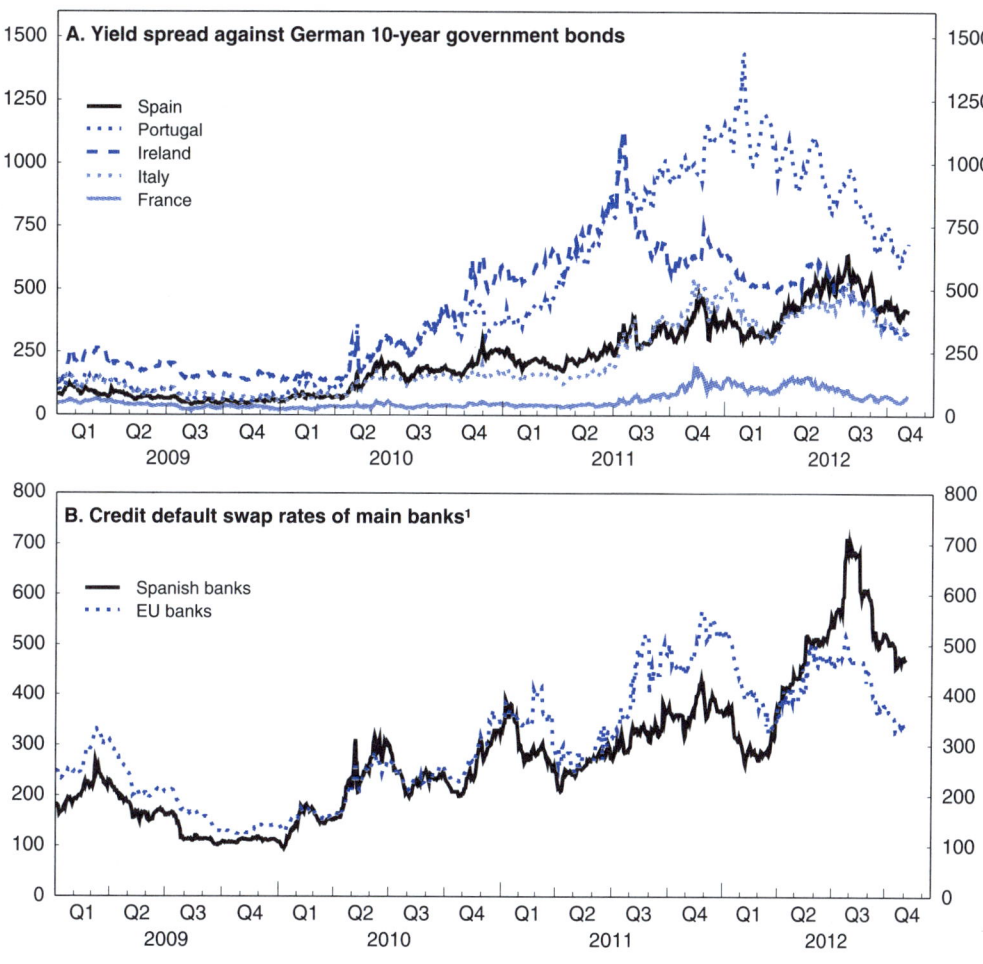

1. Credit default swaps, 5-year senior debt, mid-rate spreads between the entity and the relevant benchmark curve. Spain is an unweighted average of the four main banks. The EU average is calculated by Datastream and includes around 60 banks.

Source: Datastream Database (2012), November.

StatLink ⟶ http://dx.doi.org/10.1787/888932740214

improvements in economic performance and should be actively pursued. Beyond these immediate needs, further structural reforms are needed to raise employment and productivity performance, improve competitiveness, and reduce risks of poverty and social exclusion, notably among the young. A credible policy strategy in this area would also bolster confidence in the short term.

This *Economic Survey* examines policies to improve financial market confidence as well as structural reforms required to boost growth and reduce imbalances, and achieve fiscal consolidation. Chapter 1 discusses progress in deleveraging in the private sector and policies to redress the banking sector. This is followed by an analysis of how to facilitate the integration of young workers, one of the most challenging issues in the labour market (Chapter 2).

The economy has contracted since the third quarter of 2011 due to lower public and private consumption and investment (Figure 1). Lower spending reflects deleveraging in the private sector and budgetary consolidation, both of which are needed to eliminate imbalances. Net lending to the private non-financial sector has turned negative. The unemployment rate has risen to 24% and above 50% for youth. The adjustment of residential housing construction is well advanced, as housing starts have fallen by 90% from their 2007 level, while the number of finished houses has dropped by about 80%. The share of housing investment in GDP has fallen from 13 to 6¼ per cent, reaching historical minima, although it is still higher than in many OECD economies. Export performance has been relatively strong. Relative unit labour costs have fallen since 2009 on the back of sharp productivity gains. These gains are mainly explained by cuts in low-productivity jobs, mostly temporary and construction sector jobs and further gains depends on the ability of finding new sources of productivity growth. In fact, employment costs accelerated in 2011, reflecting inertia in wage setting, including indexation to past inflation. Nevertheless, newly signed contracts stipulate considerably lower wage growth.

Overall, further output and employment losses are projected in 2012 and 2013, while inflation is expected to be subdued after a VAT-related spike in prices in the 3rd quarter of 2012 (Table 1). There are downward risks to the projection in 2013 if access to private external funding remains tight and capital outflows continue. Public debt may differ from

Table 1. **Short-term economic outlook**[1]

| | Current prices, EUR billion | Percentage change, volume | | | | | |
| | | Outcomes | | | Projections | | |
	2008	2009	2010	2011	2012	2013	2014
Gross domestic product	1 087.7	-3.7	-0.3	0.4	-1.3	-1.4	0.5
Private consumption	622.4	-3.8	0.7	-1.0	-1.9	-2.3	-0.5
Government consumption	212.0	3.8	1.5	-0.5	-4.1	-4.0	-0.8
Gross fixed capital formation	312.0	-18.0	-6.2	-5.3	-9.1	-9.0	-2.7
of which: Residential	117.8	-23.1	-10.1	-6.7	-6.7	-4.4	-2.7
Final domestic demand	1 146.4	-6.2	-0.8	-1.8	-3.9	-4.0	-0.9
Stockbuilding[2]	4.7	0.0	0.1	-0.1	-0.0	0.0	0.0
Total domestic demand	1 151.1	-6.3	-0.6	-1.9	-3.9	-4.0	-0.9
Exports of goods and services	288.2	-10.0	11.3	7.6	4.0	6.4	6.2
Imports of goods and services	351.5	-17.2	9.2	-0.9	-4.5	-1.3	2.4
Net exports[2]	-63.3	2.9	0.3	2.3	2.6	2.5	1.4
Memorandum items:							
GDP deflator	..	0.1	0.4	1.0	0.3	0.7	0.4
Harmonised index of consumer prices (HICP)	..	-0.2	2.0	3.1	2.2	1.2	0.4
Core HICP (excluding food and energy)	..	0.9	0.8	1.2	1.0	0.9	0.4
Private consumption deflator	..	-1.1	2.0	2.9	2.2	0.8	0.3
Unemployment rate	..	18.0	20.1	21.6	25.0	26.9	26.8
Household saving ratio[3]	..	17.8	13.1	11.0	9.3	7.7	7.7
General government							
Financial balance[4]	..	-11.2	-9.7	-9.4	-8.1	-6.3	-5.9
Gross debt[4]	..	62.9	67.7	76.9	93.8	100.2	105.3
Gross debt (Maastricht definition)[4]	..	53.9	61.5	69.3	86.1	92.6	97.6
Current account balance[4]	..	-4.8	-4.5	-3.5	-2.0	0.5	1.8

1. National accounts are based on official chain-linked data which introduces a discrepancy between real demand components and GDP. For further details see *OECD Economic Outlook*, "Sources and Methods" at *www.oecd.org/eco/sources-and-methods*.
2. Contributions to changes in real GDP (per cent of real GDP in previous year), actual amounts in first column.
3. Defined in gross terms, per cent of disposable income.
4. Per cent of GDP.
Source: OECD (2012), OECD Economic Outlook: Statistics and OECD Economic Outlook 92 Database, November.

what is projected here, owing to uncertainty concerning the extent of bank recapitalisation by the government. On current rules, European funds to recapitalise banks are included in public debt and the transfer of impaired legacy assets to an asset management company (AMC) is foreseen to be largely funded by debt issued by the AMC and guaranteed by the government.

The current account deficit has fallen markedly but the trade balance will need to improve further

Both falling imports and rising exports (Figure 3, Panel B) have markedly narrowed the current account deficit (Figure 3, Panels A and B) and the net foreign liability position of the economy has stabilised, though at a high level of close to 90% of GDP. This position reflects net financial liabilities, whereas the foreign direct investment balance is broadly balanced (Figure 4). To some extent, the improvement in the trade balance reflects the impact of the output gap (which is larger than in main trading partners) on the trade balance. The cyclically-adjusted trade balance is therefore likely to be currently in deficit even though the actual balance was in surplus in the second quarter of 2012. Export performance held up relatively well compared to the other large economies of the euro area since the introduction of the common currency (see also OECD, 2010a for a discussion of related issues). In recent years Spain has gained market share (export performance has improved since 2008, as illustrated in Figure 1), part of these gains being explained by improved cost competitiveness, with unit labour costs falling in all sectors, notably in the manufacturing sector.

The high net foreign liability position will need to fall to reduce vulnerabilities. Assuming trend nominal GDP growth of 3% (broadly consistent with the current estimate of potential growth of the OECD), a current account deficit of less than 3% of GDP would be needed to begin reducing it. Moreover, even if the nominal return on net foreign liabilities were contained at 4½ per cent in future years, which is still above the current average return on foreign liabilities observed in 2012, the trade surplus may need to stay above 1%.

Restoring banks' access to funding is the most urgent priority

Wholesale funding conditions have also deteriorated substantially, including in the largest, internationally diversified banks which are only modestly exposed to domestic credit and the housing market, although the situation improved somewhat following the announcement, in September 2012, of the new unlimited bond-buying programme (OMT) in the context of an EFSF or ESM programme.

Credit ratings of banks depend to a large extent on sovereign ratings. The reduced value of the implicit government guarantee results in poorer funding conditions. Conversely the risks to government finances resulting from implicit guarantees led to a deterioration in sovereign ratings (Schich and Kim, 2012). Domestic retail funding appears to have broadly held up so far. A contained trend decline in deposits held by the domestic private non financial sector reflects to some extent household financial investments in government debt and commercial paper, declining gross household financial wealth and fluctuations in typically volatile business deposits. However, as the experience of Greece and, more recently, Italy shows, more significant reductions in deposits could occur, and deposits of non-residents have declined significantly.

Figure 3. **Developments in the balance of payments**

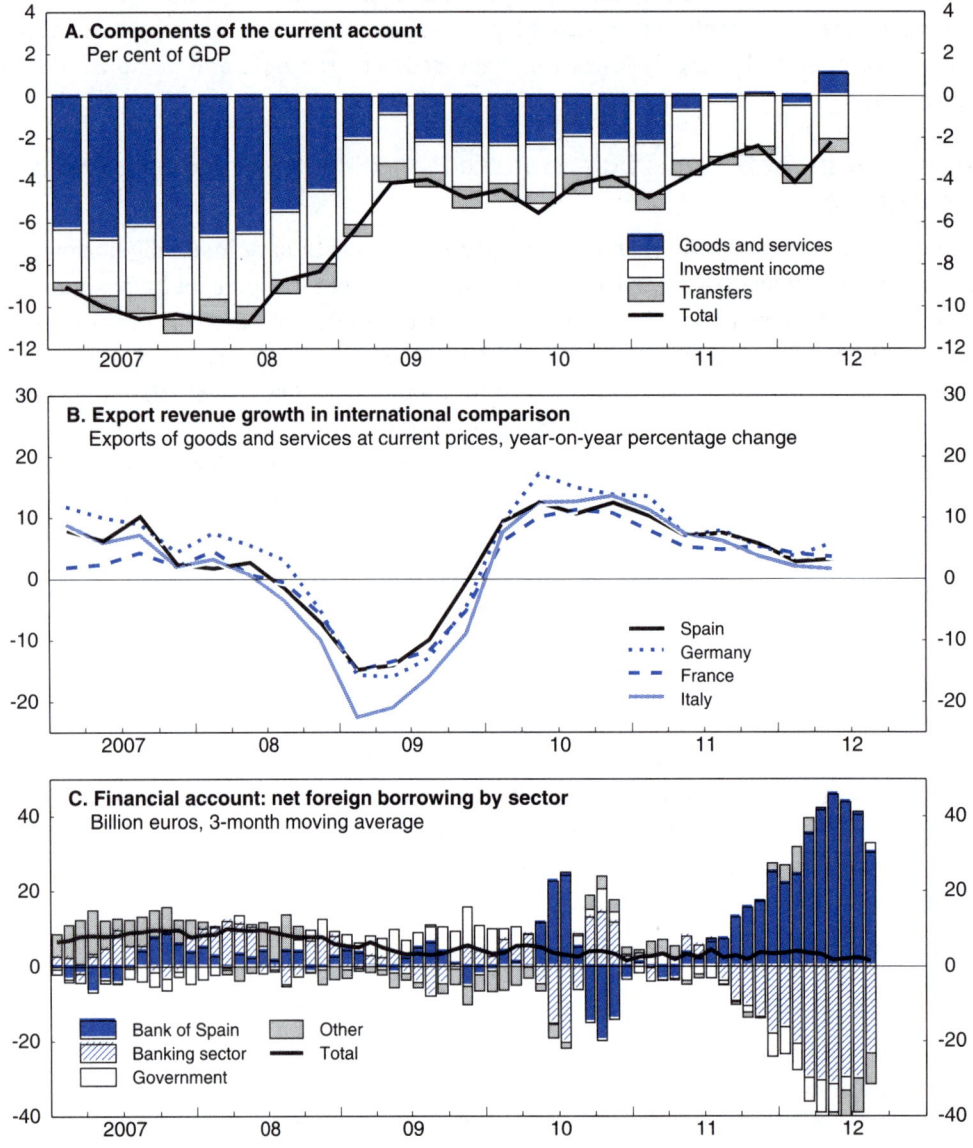

Source: OECD (2012), *OECD Economic Outlook: Statistics and Projections Database*, November; and Banco de España (2012), *Boletín Estadístico Database*, November.

StatLink ⟨⟩ http://dx.doi.org/10.1787/888932740233

The ratio of doubtful loans (non-performing loans and loans which are performing but for which there are doubts as to repayment prospects) accelerated. This ratio is expected to rise further as economic activity continues to decline. Despite falling net lending, private sector debt burdens relative to GDP have been diminishing only slowly since they peaked in 2008, and remain high in international comparison, especially in the non-financial business sector. To a considerable extent, this reflects low growth of nominal GDP in comparison to countries which have deleveraged more quickly. For household mortgages, doubtful loan ratios have remained low so far, in part reflecting some regulatory safeguards taken in the boom period, as well as the prevalence of variable-rate mortgages and high net wealth relative to income by historical standards.

Figure 4. **Net foreign asset position and gross external debt**

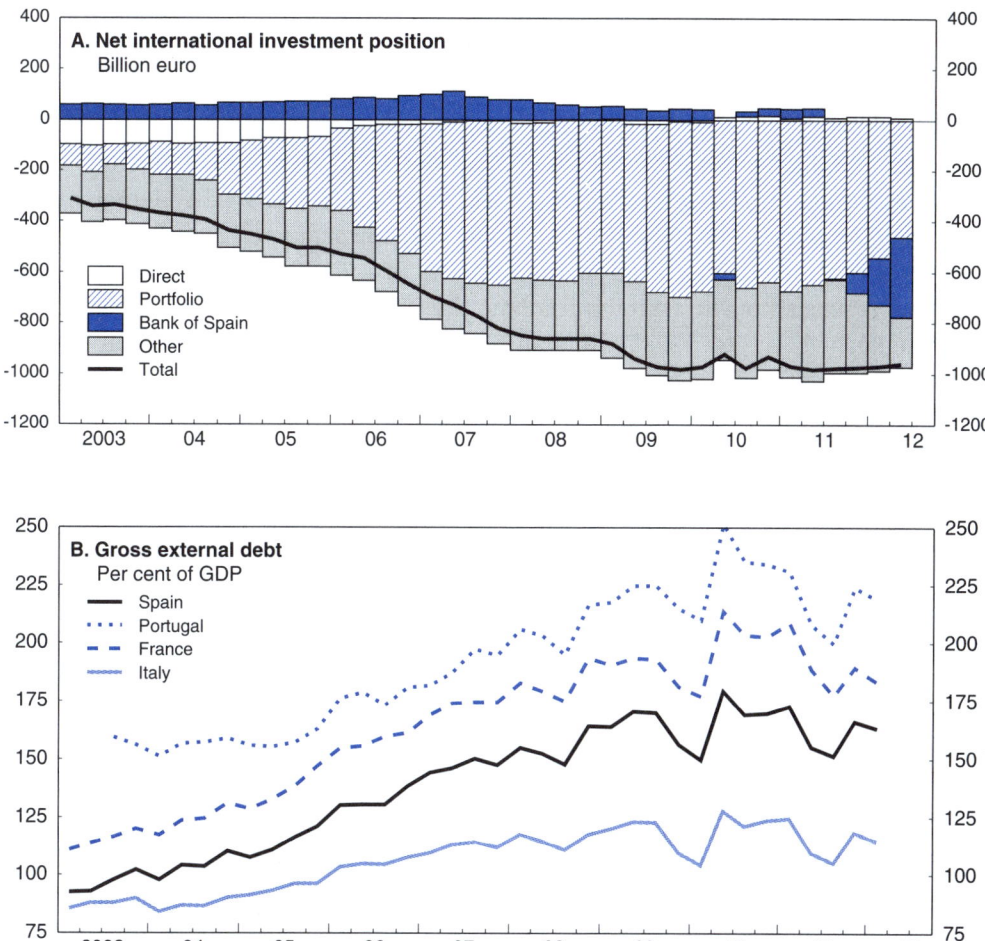

Source: Banco de España (2012), *Indicadores Económicos Database*; World Bank (2012), Quarterly External Debt Statistics (World DataBank); and OECD (2012), *OECD Economic Outlook: Statistics and Projections Database*, November.

StatLink ᵐˢᴾ *http://dx.doi.org/10.1787/888932740252*

The banks' total exposure to real estate development (including repossessed real estate) reached 28½ per cent of GDP at end-2011, of which half was classified as "problematic" (that is, doubtful loans, loans showing more general weakness in repayment prospects as well as foreclosed assets). To accelerate loss recognition on real estate exposures the government has required banks to build up buffers worth about 45% of the total exposure to real estate development, which have to be in place by June 2013. While these buffers were assessed to be broadly adequate in the recent *Financial Sector Assessment Programme* (IMF, 2012), the policy has not stabilised financial market confidence, in view of the impact of the ongoing recession on banks assets more generally.

The government asked for an independent detailed stress-test on the whole portfolio of individual banks, which was conducted between June and September 2012. Under an adverse scenario, involving a significantly worse macroeconomic outlook than is currently projected, 7 banking groups representing 38% of the banking sector would need 53.8 billion euros (5% of GDP) more capital, once ongoing mergers (and some tax effects) are taken into account, and 59 billion euros without considering projected mergers. The stress testing exercise has been comprehensive and takes into account detailed information of balance sheets and loan portfolios of individual banks. It has been conducted under the supervision of European Union institutions (The European Commission, the ECB and the European Banking Authority) and the International Monetary Fund, and provides a solid assessment of the capital needs.

Up to 100 billion euros (9½ per cent of Spanish GDP) from a loan obtained from euro area governments may be used to cover capital shortfalls. Based on the Memorandum of Understanding agreed on 20 July, by end-October 2012 the banks will have to present plans to meet capital needs identified in the analysis of individual bank balance sheets, specifying requested public capital injections. These plans must be implemented by June 2013. The Spanish authorities should stand ready to react in the future if the economic situation deteriorates significantly beyond the prudent stress test assumptions.

Steps have been taken to accelerate the restructuring and resolution of banks

To stabilise the banking system and restart lending, the authorities need to promptly recapitalise viable banks in need of capital, as set out in the Memorandum of Understanding, while quickly resolving non-viable banks (see *e.g.* Bouis and Cournède, 2012). The lack of incentives for weak banks to recognise losses could slow the reallocation of credit and resources to productive use. It could also undermine confidence in the financial system as a whole owing to the financial links between the banks. With hindsight, several banks were resolved orderly too late, only in 2011. Numerous weak savings banks were merged into large institutions, supported by the government, even as late as 2012, and the financial market reform legislated in May reintroduced some incentives for banks to merge.

Mergers may not raise efficiency and can create large, weak institutions, aggravating issues of too big to fail. In fact, some merged institutions have themselves had to be resolved orderly or nationalised eventually, notably the 4th largest banking group, BFA, which the government has nationalised. In orderly resolving non-viable banks, mergers of weak banks should therefore be avoided. Government recapitalisation will be based on the needs identified by the independent assessments of individual bank balance sheets in order to ensure the adequacy of capital buffers. This avoids the perception of soft budget constraints in partially or fully nationalised banks.

Bank resolution procedures were reformed in 2009 but continued to fall short of the Key Attributes of Effective Resolution Regimes for Financial Institutions issued by the Financial Stability Board. As required by the Memorandum of Understanding, the Spanish authorities introduced legislation to notably accelerate resolution of non-viable banks in August 2012. This legislation is welcome. The legislation should be used to override shareholder rights, for example, to avoid that incumbent shareholders hold up decisions of the resolution authorities on the transfer of assets of banks subject to resolution and to impose losses on creditors. However, the new legislation specifies that losses be imposed on owners of hybrid capital and subordinated debt instruments only but not on senior debt. The Memorandum of Understanding also provides a timetable for restructuring and addressing viable banks' capital needs, with all significant capital needs met by end-2012, and for orderly resolving non-viable banks. It foresees transferring impaired legacy assets to an asset management company, and measures to strengthen the supervisory and regulatory framework to improve crisis prevention in the future.

The separation of legacy assets from all banks in need of public support in a dedicated asset management company, as foreseen in the programme, should improve confidence in the banks and focus bank management on the lending and deposit-taking business. The legislation requires that private capital contributes to the funding of the asset management company. However, most funding needs will be covered with the issuance of bonds guaranteed by the Spanish government, which exposes government finances to financial risks. It is therefore important that legacy assets transferred are conservatively priced. The Memorandum of Understanding foresees that legacy assets be priced at "long-term economic value" which risks pricing them above what current market conditions warrant. A relatively high transfer price also risks reducing the extent to which bank creditors take losses, even though the Key Attributes of Effective Resolution Regimes (Financial Stability Board, 2011) require only that owners of bank debt should not recover more funds than they would in case of liquidation. Legacy assets transferred to the asset management company should be conservatively priced. Another option would be to use bank debt that has been selected for loss absorption (see below) to help fund the transfer of assets from a bank with solvency problems to the asset management company.

Resolution of non-viable banks needs to impose losses to some creditors to protect tax-payers better

To protect the taxpayers and avoid aggravating feedback loops between government finances and the financial systems, some bank creditors should be forced to bear losses in the current crisis, as foreseen in the Memorandum of Understanding. Previously losses emerging in the resolution of insolvent banks were largely been borne by the deposit insurance fund, which is funded and managed by the banking sector. Losses born solely through the deposit insurance fund could impose a heavy burden on viable banks through their contributions to the deposit insurance fund. If the government were to take a larger share of these losses, this would risk impairing financial confidence further as it would deteriorate the fiscal position. Moreover, in both cases moral hazard is aggravated. Forcing bank creditors to assume losses in the context of bank resolution, as foreseen in the Memorandum of Understanding is, hence, welcome. So far, equity holders have generally been wiped out, while subordinate debt holders have been protected in full (Schich and Lindh, 2012), although such debt is contractually required to absorb losses in the event of bankruptcy.

A first option would be to require only holders of subordinated debt and lower-ranked hybrid capital to take losses (also called "bailing-in"), as foreseen in the Memorandum of Understanding, especially since *Basel III* solvency requirements emphasise the role of higher-quality capital, making the issuance of subordinate debt less important in future. Banks have substantial amounts of subordinated debt outstanding, amounting to 83 billion euros at end-2011 (8% of GDP). This policy should also be applied to absorb losses of banks which are recapitalised by the government rather than resolved orderly.

As many banks have sold preferential shares and subordinate debt to their retail customers, without necessarily providing transparent information about the risks, smaller haircuts need to be imposed on such investors in the interests of consumer protection. Even so, it should be noted that about half of subordinate debt issued by Spanish banks has been subscribed by institutional investors, where consumer protection concerns do not apply, offering ample room to apply bailing-in to these investors. To prevent recurrence of such practices in the future, it is important to investigate responsibilities of bank management in breaking consumer protection rules and review the effectiveness of consumer protection rules. Steps to limit the sale of hybrid capital instruments to private households were taken in legislation introduced in August 2012.

Banks have recently reduced hybrid capital and subordinated debt buffers by buying back such instruments or transforming them in part into deposits, perhaps in order to protect their relationships with clients or raise reported profits. This may have reduced the availability of these instruments for loss absorption, including in cases where such instruments are held by institutional investors. The authorities should be proactive in preventing any payouts or repurchases of capital when the capacity of loss-absorption is compromised. By contrast, their conversion in equity is desirable. Banks' operations reducing their hybrid capital and subordinated debt buffers should be closely supervised and stopped if these operations reduce the amount of funds which may be needed for absorbing losses. The bank supervisor, the *Banco de España*, needs to be endowed with the powers to take such action. Moreover, the provision in Memorandum of Understanding, which requires the *Banco de España* to stop banks which may need public support from repurchasing such debt instruments at above market price +10% may not be satisfactory, as market conditions may be difficult to observe and market prices depend on the announced bail-in policy. Contagion risks could also be reduced by giving depositors strict preference over other types of bank creditors. It is also appropriate to fund remaining costs of bank resolution with contributions paid by the banks, spread over time. These contributions, which should be separated from the contributions to deposit insurance, should be assessed on the total of bank balance sheets.

Potential fiscal costs could be reduced further by imposing losses on senior debt, in addition to subordinated debt, for banks in orderly resolution procedures. Such a bail-in would need to be carefully designed (IMF, 2012b). Contagion risks may be limited in a context of comprehensive bank restructuring, in which all non-viable banks are orderly resolved and viable banks with capital needs comprehensively recapitalised.

Reform of bankruptcy procedures can accelerate restructuring

Effective mechanisms to deal with bankruptcies among non-financial businesses and private households can accelerate the recognition of losses on loans that creditors cannot repay and can help to reallocate resources to productive use (IMF, 2002). These mechanisms appear to be relatively poorly developed in Spain (Mora and Fuentes, 2012 and references therein). Recourse to judicial bankruptcy proceedings is much lower than in other high-income economies. The procedures appear to be relatively slow and expected costs for entrepreneurs from undergoing such procedures are unusually high, in part reflecting personal liability clauses which are unusual in other countries and the absence of the possibility of full discharge of over-indebted creditors ("fresh start") in most cases. Creditors' recovery of loans from firms undergoing bankruptcy appears to be relatively low, although few firms appear to avoid liquidation and survive on the back of restructuring of their debt (Mora and Fuentes, 2012 and references therein). Bankruptcy proceedings for non-financial businesses should be reformed to raise their efficiency. For example, steps could be taken to accelerate judicial proceedings and to reduce expected costs to managers by limiting the threat of sanctions and widening the applicability of debt discharge. The government is planning to review bankruptcy legislation in order to address shortcomings in bankruptcy procedures for firms, which is welcome.

Ineffective bankruptcy rules may also hold back productivity performance in the longer term by biasing investment decisions (Mora and Fuentes, 2012 and references therein). Firms and their lenders in Spain may avoid the bankruptcy system by making extensive use of the mortgage system, which provides more effective protection to creditors. Ineffective bankruptcy rules may therefore strengthen incentives to invest in assets that can serve as mortgage collateral, notably construction and real estate, to the detriment of investment in assets which cannot serve as collateral, such as human capital or technological know-how, even if such investments are more profitable.

Box 1. Key recommendations to exit the banking crisis

- Viable banks with capital needs should be recapitalised promptly based on the capital needs identified by independent assessments of individual bank balance sheets and non-viable banks should be resolved in an orderly manner as soon as possible, as foreseen in the Memorandum of Understanding.

- Holders of subordinated debt and lower-ranked hybrid capital instruments should absorb losses of banks that are resolved or are recapitalised by the government, as foreseen in the Memorandum of Understanding, and financial operations of banks reducing the amount of loss-absorbing bank debt should be prevented. Where consumer protection concerns exist, smaller losses may be imposed on retail investors.

The government has introduced large front-loaded budget consolidation

The general government deficit of 9.4% of GDP in 2011 overshot the original target agreed with the EU by 3.4 percentage points. This figure includes ½ percentage point of expenditure reflecting financial support to banks that can be considered of a one-off nature. The overrun occurred mostly due to weaker revenue than expected, whereas the consolidation commitments undertaken in 2010, which focused on spending reductions (OECD, 2010a), were largely kept. Non-interest government spending fell significantly (Table 2). Most of the deviation from the target occurred at regional government level, in part because regional governments were hit by falling revenues from housing transactions, which fully accrue to them, and because of the rigidity of education and health spending, which account for a large share of their budgets (see OECD, 2010a for a review of budgetary policy issues at regional government level). To some extent the sensitivity of tax revenues to domestic demand reflects the characteristics of the tax structure, with higher VAT rates applying to consumer durables, the sales of which have fallen particularly strongly. The strong transmission of fluctuations in output to employment, which is relatively heavily taxed (see below), also plays a role.

In view of the deficit overrun and deteriorating growth prospects, the government agreed new deficit objectives with the European Union on 10 July 2012 (Table 3). The delay by one year to meet the 3% deficit target is a welcome decision as trying to meet it despite a deteriorating economic situation would have been self-defeating. The national targets have been distributed across the levels of government. The contribution of regional governments to budget consolidation is important because they account for about 35% of general government spending. Hence all levels of government will need to make a substantial contribution to consolidation.

Table 2. **General government revenue and expenditure**
Per cent of GDP

	2000	2007	2010	2011
Total revenue	38.2	41.1	36.6	35.7
Total current revenue	37.6	40.6	36.5	35.8
Households taxes	7.1	8.2	7.6	7.6
Corporate taxes	3.2	4.8	1.9	1.9
Indirect taxes	11.4	11.6	10.5	9.9
Social security contributions	12.9	13.0	13.4	13.2
Other current revenue	3.1	3.0	3.2	3.2
Capital revenue	0.6	0.5	0.0	-0.1
Total expenditure	39.2	39.2	46.3	45.2
Total current expenditure	36.1	35.4	43.0	42.9
Government consumption	17.1	18.3	21.4	20.9
Social security benefits	12.0	11.6	15.4	15.4
Interest/property income paid	3.2	1.6	1.9	2.5
Other expenditure	3.7	3.8	4.2	4.1
Gross saving	1.5	5.2	-6.4	-7.2
Capital expenditure	3.1	3.8	3.3	2.2
Investment	3.2	4.0	4.0	2.9
Capital transfers	-0.1	-0.2	-0.7	-0.7
Net lending	-1.0	1.9	-9.7	-9.4
Gross debt (Maastricht definition)	59.4	36.3	61.5	69.3
Structural budget items, as a per cent of potential GDP				
Structural current spending	37.3	37.0	40.2	39..8
Structural current revenues	37.7	40.6	36.4	35.7
Structural balance	-2.1	0.3	-6.6	-5.5
Structural primary current spending	34.0	35.4	38.4	37.5
Structural primary balance	0.8	1.4	-5.4	-4.4
Memorandum items:				
Potential output growth	3.9	3.1	1.4	1.3
Output gap	2.7	2.7	-5.4	-6.1

Source: OECD (2012), OECD Economic Outlook: Statistics and Projections Database, November.

Table 3. **Fiscal targets 2012-14 for general government**
In per cent of GDP

	2011[1]	2012	2013	2014
General government financial balance	-9.4	-6.3	-4.5	-2.8
of which: Autonomous regions	-3.3	-1.5	-0.7	-0.1

1. Budget outcome.
Source: Ministerio de Hacienda y Administraciones Públicas.

Meeting these deficit targets could allow public debt to stabilise relative to GDP by around 2014. According to OECD estimates, the targets require a reduction of the primary structural budget balance of 4% of GDP in 2012 and 2½ per cent in 2013, assuming economic activity evolves broadly as projected in Table 1. A further consolidation effort of 1¾ per cent of GDP is needed in 2014 even if GDP grows in line with potential (estimated at 1.2% by the OECD). If growth turns out somewhat smaller, as projected, consolidation needs may be somewhat larger. The structural consolidation needs are smaller according to the Spanish authorities owing to different assumptions on potential growth of the economy. In any case, the new targets remain challenging, given the macroeconomic context. Meeting the headline deficit target for 2014 will involve a large structural surplus according to OECD estimations of the output gap (which are larger than the estimates of the Spanish authorities). According to estimates of the government, the headline deficit target in 2014 is still projected to imply a structural deficit of 1.7% of GDP.

Budgetary measures introduced this year and next broadly match the consolidation needs in 2012 and 2013 estimated by the OECD (Table 4). The consolidation package announced in July 2012 includes significant tax increases, notably a 3 percentage point rise in the standard VAT rate to 21% while the 8% rate is raised to 10%, and the lowest rate remains at 4%. Some goods and services are also moved from the 8% rate to the standard rate. Cuts in expenditures are also significant, with notably the disappearance of the 14th month of salary for public employees in 2012 (except for workers earning less than 962 euros per month), the public employment freeze and a reduction in public employees' sickness benefits as well as a reduction in the unemployment benefit replacement rate for new unemployment spells from the 6th month onwards to 50%.

Table 4. **Expected improvement of the general government budget balance from measures taking effect in 2012 and 2013**

Per cent of GDP

	2012	2013
Expenditure	**2.6**	**1.8**
Public employment	0.5	-0.2
Labour market policies	0.2	0.4
Social spending other than health or education (mostly long-term care)	0.0	0.1
Other central government spending	0.8	0.4
Other specific regional government measures (may include revenue measures)	0.9	0.7
of which: Health and education spending	0.5	0.6
Reform of local government and local government measures (may include revenue measures)	0.1	0.3
Revenue	**2.2**	**0.8**
Nation-wide taxes	1.5	0.7
of which: VAT	0.1	0.8
Other indirect taxes (mostly fuel tax)	0.0	0.1
Personal income tax	0.4	0.3
Real estate tax	0.1	
Tax amnesty	0.2	-0.2
Corporate tax	0.6	-0.3
Other	0.0	0.0
Regional government revenue measures	0.5	
Social security contributions		0.2
Fight of social security fraud	0.2	
Total	**4.8**	**2.6**

Source: Ministry of Finance and Public Administration.

In August 2012, the government extended budgetary plans to the year 2014 with additional spending cuts of about 1% of GDP. A large part of these proposed savings are expected from measures that regional and local governments are expected to take to meet their deficit targets, and from a reform of local government, which is not legislated yet. Several of these measures have yet to be further specified. Measures in this order of magnitude would only offset part of the revenue losses as temporary measures introduced earlier on drop out. Temporary measures include notably the increase in personal income and real estate taxes, which are programmed to be phased out in 2014. Most of the corporate tax measures simply brings revenues forward and thus have no permanent effect. The salary cut in civil servants' pay may also not result in durable spending cuts as the salary payment will be reintroduced in 2015 as a compulsory contribution to a funded pension scheme, on the condition that the deficit targets are met. In addition, cuts in the level of public salaries are hard to sustain because they could induce hiring difficulties in the long term.

There are still risks that the budget deficit may exceed the target this year and next. In 2012 they mainly relate to the recapitalisation of banks by the government, some of which might count as expenditure, although they are one-off effects. The depressing impact of weakening domestic demand on tax revenues may in addition be underestimated. Some of the measures, notably the one-off tax amnesty, are uncertain in their budgetary effects. Additional measures are likely to be needed to meet the headline deficit target for 2014 according to OECD estimates. In any case, the measures need to be spelled out in more detail.

To improve confidence in government finances, further permanent deficit-reducing measures may need to be introduced, while minimising their regressive impact, if any, and, in any case, measures already planned specified in full, while paying careful attention to a fair burden sharing of consolidation efforts to maintain social support since fiscal consolidation episodes tend to be regressive (Ahrend *et al.*, 2011). To bolster confidence it will be important to rapidly stabilise the public debt to GDP ratio. Nevertheless, if output growth proves well below projections it would be counterproductive to offset such risks and the government should let automatic stabilisers operate, at least partially.

Ambitious budgetary rules have been introduced

National budgetary rules introduced in 2012 require the general government budget, as well as the budgets of each of the central government, the regions, the municipalities and the social security system, to be in balance structurally from 2020 onwards. They also limit the growth of government expenditure in line with recent EU rules (Box 2). The rules also strengthen central government oversight of regional governments and their budgetary reporting. The requirement to report regional budgetary data on a monthly basis will be effective from October onwards, improving rapid detection of changes in budgetary developments. Moreover, the government has set up a fund worth 18 billion euros which can lend to regional governments requiring official support to cover funding needs at their request. So far, six regional governments have announced that they will request to borrow from this fund. To avoid moral hazard, loans from the fund are subject to conditionality, along the lines of the budgetary rules described in Box 2, although regions will be subject to closer oversight by the central government and can be subjected more quickly to sanctions. It is critical that the new requirements on the publication and control of regional government budgetary policies are strictly implemented. Earlier in the year, the central government had also offered liquidity assistance for local and regional governments, subject to conditionality, to cover supplier payment arrears. Local governments have received 9.5 billion euros (0.9% of GDP) and the regions 17.7 billion euros (1.7% of GDP) under this programme.

Box 2. **New budgetary rules apply from 2012**

In April 2012, legislation came into force requiring a structural fiscal balance and limiting public debt to 60% of GDP in 2020 onwards. It also limits government spending growth to nominal national medium-term GDP growth at each level of government with immediate effect. A higher structural deficit of up to 0.4% of GDP would be allowed when structural reforms with a positive medium-term impact on the budget are implemented. The regional governments and the central government may also record a temporarily higher deficit in specific situations. By 2020 general government debt must be reduced by at least 2 percentage points of GDP per year if annual real GDP growth or net employment growth reach at least 2%, until debt falls to 60% of GDP. The general government structural deficit has to be reduced by an average of 0.8% of GDP per year, to which the central and regional governments contribute. Any administration exceeding these ceilings will be banned from issuing further net debt. The law puts stronger requirements on reporting. Budgets must be presented in national accounts terms. Budgetary outcomes have to be presented on a monthly basis by the regions and on a quarterly basis by municipalities. If the central government detects risks of non-compliance it can issue an early warning, after which the administration concerned has one month to take action. If actions taken are deemed insufficient, the central government can intervene by, for example, withdrawing the authorisation for the administration concerned to issue debt, or intervening in discretionary spending and revenue decisions.

If an annual target is not met a plan has to be developed to correct the deviation within one year. If that plan is not met, a sanction regime applies. The administration breaching the target will not have access to additional credit and will have to deposit 0.2% of its nominal GDP at the Bank of Spain. These funds can only be withdrawn once corrective measures are implemented. If this is not done within 3 months, the administration will have to pay interest on the deposit and after another 3 months it becomes a fine. Moreover, a "no bail out" clause applies, according to which higher-ranking levels of government may not assume the commitments of lower ranking ones.

The newly introduced fiscal rules have the potential to substantially improve the commitment to reach the target of a balanced budget and it is advisable to allow some experience to accumulate before considering substantial changes. In the meantime, the authorities could consider potential improvements to be introduced at a later stage. Steps can be taken to improve the design of budgetary rules by offsetting deficit overruns with additional consolidation measures in subsequent years. In the "debt brake" rules in Germany and Switzerland, such overruns are booked in a compensation account. If its balance exceeds a set threshold it must be reduced over time. Specific budgetary rules would be useful for the central and regional governments, where control of structural budget balances over the cycle is especially important.

As a complementary tool to the introduction of fiscal rules, the government should set up an independent fiscal council, as required in the recommendations adopted by the Council of the European Union. Such a fiscal council should notably provide the government and the public with independent analysis of the impact of fiscal policy, including through independent fiscal projections at all levels of government. It could also exercise more normative mandates so as to help reduce the pro-cyclicality of fiscal policy and reinforce fiscal discipline on all levels of government. Such a body could help "depoliticise" decisions to sanction regional governments that have not abided by the rules. For it to be effective in this role, the fiscal council needs to be designed as a truly independent body, which is unelected, but accountable, and with a term structure for its management board which does not coincide with the political cycle. It should be included in fiscal policy formulation and in the monitoring process. The government should be required to consider the recommendations by the agency and if it chooses not to follow the recommendations of the new fiscal council, the government should be required to publically justify its actions (Hagemann, 2010).

Pension reform has damped the expected increase in ageing-related spending but further reform is necessary

Pension spending as a share of GDP had been due to increase from 10% of GDP in 2010 to 16½ per cent of GDP by 2060. However, the pension reforms introduced in 2011 are expected to reduce the projected increase in annual pension spending from 6½ per cent of GDP to about 3% of GDP, in part by raising the legal retirement age to 67 for workers who have contribution periods shorter than 38.5 years (see MinEH, 2011a for more details). This estimate of future pension spending assumes that the parameters of the pension system will be adjusted in such a way as to offset the impact on pension spending of further increases in life expectancy from 2027 onwards. However, no specific adjustment has yet been proposed. Without it, pension spending is projected to rise by 3.6% of GDP by 2060. An indexation formula linking pension system parameters to changes in life expectancy should be introduced as soon as possible. The expected increase in health and long-term care spending, while subject to more uncertainty, is estimated at 2% of GDP. It is expected to be partly offset by a fall in education and unemployment spending of 1.6% of GDP. Savings in future pension spending can be achieved by reforming survivors' pension benefits in the light of high labour market participation of young women, by focusing such benefits more closely to cases of need, as recommended in the 2010 OECD Economic Surveys. Such steps would also improve the fairness of the pension system.

Despite the 2011 pension reform, the pension system continues to generate unnecessary disincentives to supply labour in the formal economy. In particular, in the reformed system, which applies to all workers entering the labour market, pension benefits are determined by the level of earnings in the last 25 years before retirement and the maximum pension entitlement is attained after 37 years of contributions. These settings do not sufficiently acknowledge long contributory careers, penalise people with stable earnings throughout their working lives and do not incentivise extending working lives after the relevant periods of contributions have been attained. These settings encourage workers and their employers to only partially declare earnings before they reach the last 25 years of the active working life, and not to declare any revenues in some years. The accrual rate in the pension system should be lowered so as to require a longer contribution record to obtain the full pension entitlement at the legal retirement age. Earnings throughout active working life should be assessed for the calculation of pension benefits. These steps would also help further moderate the projected increase in pension spending.

There is also scope to further reduce effective public subsidies to early retirement through extended unemployment benefit payments, although these measures should be considered as relatively low priority at present, in view of the difficult situation in the labour market, the low budgetary cost of the benefits concerned and the low educational attainment of many unemployed older workers, which limits the resulting loss in potential output. By contrast remaining partial retirement subsidies are paid to workers in employment who reduce their hours worked. These are costly to the budget so should be eliminated as soon as possible.

Budgetary consolidation should be combined with a reform of the tax system, notably to make it more green-growth friendly

Since 2010 substantial measures have been taken to reduce government expenditure. These measures have included reductions in government employment, wage cuts, and reductions in public investment and transfers. Most recently, they have also included cuts in education and health spending. Scope for achieving substantial and sustainable spending cuts within a relatively short period of time may now be reduced and the efficiency savings from public sector reform may take more time to materialise. Public spending is relatively low by international standards (Figure 5), despite high unemployment benefit spending. Government spending on health and education as a share of GDP is modest in international comparison, and OECD indicators of efficiency of health care systems across OECD countries (Joumard et al., 2010) point to relatively efficient use of the public resources in health services. Public health insurance and policies to foster access to education are key instruments to reduce inequality (Joumard et al., 2012). Cuts in the coverage provided by public insurance may result in the expansion of private health insurance without appropriate equalisation

Figure 5. **Government expenditure and tax revenue in selected OECD countries**
Per cent of GDP

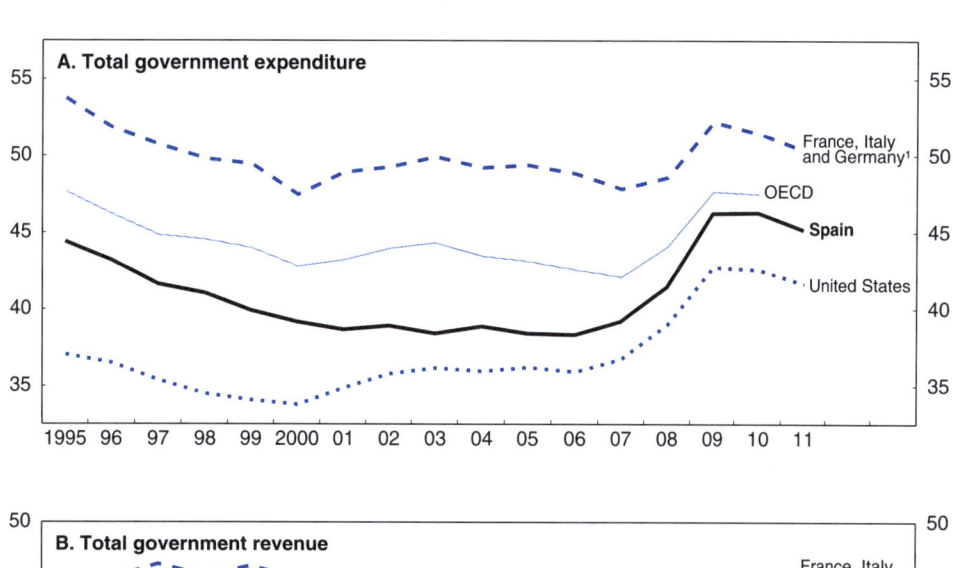

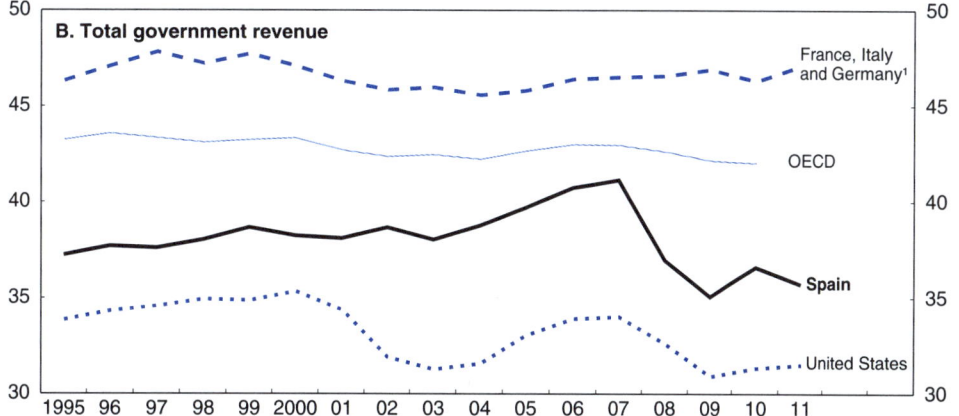

1. Unweighted averages. For the OECD aggregate 2010 is an estimate and Chile, Japan, Mexico and Turkey are excluded.
   Source: OECD (2012), OECD National Accounts Statistics Database, November.

StatLink ᴹᴵᴺ http://dx.doi.org/10.1787/888932740271

mechanisms, which can result in higher total health care costs and inequality. Reducing inequality also calls for room to be made for expanding access to education (see below). In this context, the tax-raising measures announced on 13 July to achieve further budgetary consolidation are welcome. In the near term, tax increases are likely to have less negative impacts on activity than expenditure cuts. However, tax measures need to be designed in a growth-friendly way. While the government package appropriately relies mostly on consumption taxes, some further improvements could be made (see below).

The Spanish tax system remains relatively heavily geared towards the taxation of labour, notably through social security contributions (Table 5). A reduction of employers' social security contributions would be welcome. By contrast, indirect tax revenue has been

Table 5. **Structure of tax revenue**
In per cent of GDP
Tax revenue by sector as a percentage of total tax revenues, 2010[1]

	Personal income tax	Corporate income tax	Social security contributions	Property tax	Goods and services tax	Other taxes
Spain	**21.7**	**5.5**	**37.7**	**6.1**	**26.7**	**2.2**
Australia	37.4	18.7	0.0	9.6	29.1	5.2
Austria	22.5	4.6	34.5	1.3	28.0	9.1
Belgium	28.1	6.2	32.5	6.9	25.4	0.9
Canada	35.0	10.7	15.3	11.3	24.4	3.3
Chile[2]	38.4	..	6.9	3.6	51.3	-0.3
Czech Republic	10.3	9.8	44.7	1.3	33.4	0.6
Denmark	50.6	5.7	2.1	4.0	31.7	5.9
Estonia	16.0	4.0	38.7	1.1	39.8	0.5
Finland	29.7	6.0	29.8	2.7	31.5	0.3
France	16.9	4.9	38.8	8.5	25.0	5.8
Germany	24.4	4.2	39.1	2.3	29.5	0.5
Greece[2]	22.3	..	34.6	5.6	37.1	0.4
Hungary	18.0	3.3	30.7	3.1	42.8	2.1
Iceland	35.5	4.6	11.6	6.8	35.5	5.9
Ireland	27.0	9.2	20.3	5.6	36.9	1.2
Israel	19.1	9.0	17.2	9.6	40.0	5.1
Italy	27.2	6.5	31.5	4.7	25.8	4.2
Japan	20.0	9.6	40.9	10.1	19.1	0.3
Korea	14.3	13.9	22.8	11.4	33.9	3.3
Luxembourg	21.4	14.4	29.6	7.2	27.1	0.3
Mexico[2]	28.6	..	16.7	1.7	50.2	2.7
Netherlands	22.7	5.3	36.1	3.9	30.7	1.2
New Zealand	37.5	12.4	0.0	6.9	39.3	3.9
Norway	23.8	22.6	22.8	2.9	28.0	0.0
Poland	14.6	7.2	35.7	3.9	37.0	1.6
Portugal	17.9	9.1	28.8	3.8	39.6	0.8
Slovak Republic	8.2	9.0	43.3	1.5	36.4	1.6
Slovenia	15.2	5.0	40.3	1.6	37.3	0.6
Sweden	28.0	7.6	25.0	2.4	29.5	7.6
Switzerland	32.3	10.8	23.3	7.4	21.8	4.4
Turkey	14.1	7.3	24.5	4.1	47.9	2.1
United Kingdom	28.7	8.7	19.1	12.1	30.9	0.5
United States	32.0	10.9	26.2	12.9	17.9	0.0
OECD	24.7	8.4	26.6	5.5	32.5	2.3

1. 2009 for Australia, Japan, Mexico, the Netherlands, Poland and the OECD aggregate.
2. Data shown in the first column covers both personal and corporate income tax.
Source: OECD (2012), "Revenue Statistics: Comparative Tables", *OECD Tax Statistics Database*, August.

relatively low so far. Taxation of personal income and labour earnings is more harmful for economic activity and employment than the taxation of the consumption of goods and services. Steps to broaden the VAT tax base are particularly welcome as VAT has been considerably less broad-based than in a majority of OECD countries (Figure 6), which tends to raise distortions. In 2012, several goods and services have been moved to the standard tax rate. However, a number of sectors continue to benefit from substantially reduced rates and the VAT tax base should be broadened further, moving most goods and services to the full rate. For example, tourism-related services and transport services are only taxed at 10%. Some paper products are only taxed at 4%.

Figure 6. **VAT revenue ratio**[1]
2010[2]

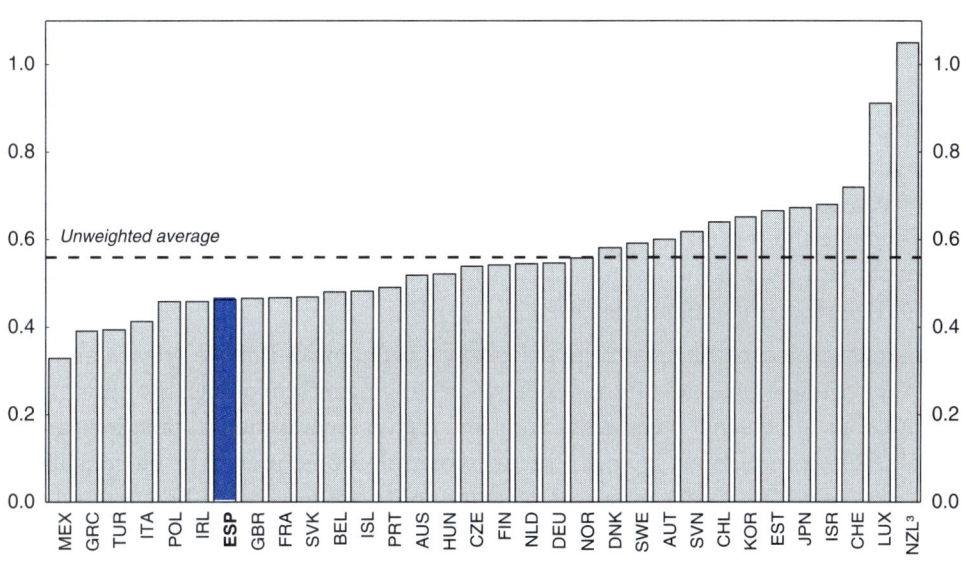

1. The VAT revenue ratio (VRR) is defined as the ratio between the actual value added tax (VAT) revenue collected and the revenue that would theoretically be raised if VAT was applied at the standard rate to all final consumption. This ratio gives an indication of the efficiency of the VAT regime in a country compared to a standard norm. It is calculated as: VRR = VAT revenue/([consumption – VAT revenue] × standard VAT rate). Consumption is final consumption expenditure from the national accounts (heading P3).
2. 2009 for Australia, Greece, Ireland, Netherlands and Poland.
3. New Zealand raised VAT from 12.5 to 15% in October 2010 which raises the average ratio in 2010 above 1.0.
Source: OECD (2012), *OECD National Accounts Statistics* and *OECD Tax Statistics Databases*, November.

StatLink 🔗 *http://dx.doi.org/10.1787/888932740290*

There is also room to remove exemptions and deductions in the taxation of personal income. These include significant deductions for contributions to personal pension plans. These deductions should be eliminated or reduced substantially. Tax deductions for pension plans, in particular, mostly benefit middle and high income households, up to a reduction of 10 000 euros of taxable income. Any positive impact of these deductions on private household saving is likely to have been more than offset by lower government savings and the rate of return on such pension plans may be significantly lower than the interest rate on government debt. Moreover, their elimination would not affect activity adversely. The government has decided to abolish the deductibility of mortgage payments for new mortgages, as required in the recommendations adopted by the Council of the European Union, which is welcome. It has also somewhat reduced tax subsidies for existing mortgages.

Environmental taxes raise revenue worth 1.5% of GDP, considerably less than in other European tax systems, where these revenues exceed 4% of GDP in some cases. Taxation of motor vehicle use is not sufficient to price in carbon externalities (OECD, 2012b) and tax advantages are granted to diesel-engines despite the risks they pose to human health. Agriculture is exempt from most environmental taxation. Introducing a national carbon tax should be considered, including on transport fuel. The government is planning to increase taxes on fuels, which is welcome. Other pollutants are only taxed in some autonomous regions although their environmental externalities extend beyond regional borders, such as sulphur oxides and nitrogen oxide. These should be taxed at the national level.

There is also scope for raising taxation of wealth, where tax rates are low and revenues raised modest (less than 0.1% of GDP). Moreover, inheritance taxes are a tool to make wealthy households bear a higher tax burden. In Spain some inheritance tax setting powers have been devolved to the regions. Since regions have competed for the richest households, tax rates are generally low and there is a risk that tax rates are lowest in regions with the highest concentration of wealthy households. Tax rates on relatively mobile tax bases with a marked redistributive objective are more appropriately set at the central government level, although, even then, tax rates must be limited to a level that is consistent with avoiding international capital flight. Inheritance tax setting powers should be attributed to the central government in full and tax rates raised. The rise in inheritance taxes could also reduce the frequent regressive impact of fiscal consolidations (Ahrend *et al.*, 2011), fostering its public acceptance.

There is also scope for reforming the tax system to make it more growth enhancing. Part of the revenues generated from a more wide-ranging reform of VAT, the elimination of tax deductions in personal income tax and from higher environmental taxation can make room for further reductions in social security contributions, provided the consolidation targets are met. These cuts in social security contributions could be targeted at low wage earners. Such a step could strengthen employment prospects and real incomes of low-skilled workers, whose employment prospects have deteriorated particularly markedly. Reductions of employer-paid social security contributions can improve competitiveness in the near term, notably in view of the inertia in the wage bargaining system. This inertia is likely to remain in the near term even after the reforms put in place this year (see below).

Part of the revenues generated by tax-revenue raising measures could also be used to pay higher child benefits to low-income families, with the benefits made conditional on attendance of continued full-time education when children reach the age of 16, when compulsory education ends. Such a step could help reduce early school drop-outs and help fight poverty, which is highly correlated with the presence of children in households, especially in Spain, where child benefits are low. Such a step could support activity, as the marginal propensity to consume of low-income households is likely to be relatively large, especially in deleveraging episodes.

Revenues from the taxation of immobile property depend heavily on the taxation of housing transactions, which discourages labour mobility, harming labour market performance (OECD, 2010a). By contrast, recurrent taxation of real estate has been found to be a relatively non-distorting tax. The increases in real estate taxes introduced this year should therefore be made permanent. Shifting towards taxation of real estate values would encourage the mobility of workers, fostering labour market adjustment. Moreover, the assignment of transaction taxes to the regions is particularly unsuited because of the volatility of revenues. Any remaining taxation of housing transactions should be assigned to the central government, which because of its size is better able to cope with the volatile revenue stream.

Box 3. Key recommendations to put public finances on a sustainable basis and make the tax system more growth friendly

- The government should aim at meeting its new headline deficit targets, unless growth is far lower than expected, in which case the automatic stabilisers should be allowed to operate, at least partially.

- Spell out the consolidation measures needed to reach the deficit target in 2014. Minimise their regressive impact, if any, to foster the social consensus around consolidation needs.

- Strictly implement control of regional government budget policies and the new requirements on the publication of regional government budget outcomes.

- Raise taxes on environmental externalities, including on transport fuels. Apply the standard VAT tax rate to more goods and services. Consider using some of the additional revenues raised though VAT and environmental taxation to further lower social security contributions for workers on low earnings. Make increases in the taxation of real estate values permanent and reduce taxation of housing transactions.

Progress in labour market reform is considerable but important challenges remain

In the context of a still weak outlook for output growth, Spain faces very high unemployment. Segments of the population that were already at a disadvantage before the crisis – young people, immigrants and temporary workers – have borne the brunt of rising unemployment. In April 2012, the unemployment rate of those aged less than 25 was 51.5%. The percentage of youth neither in employment nor in education or training (NEET) is close to 20%, one of the highest rates in the OECD. Moreover, the proportion of unemployed who have been out of work for more than 12 months rose to 43% at the end of 2011. The experience of previous severe economic downturns suggests that it may take a long time to absorb the large pool of unemployed.

The main challenges for the Spanish labour market are therefore to deal with very high labour market slack and to prevent unemployment from becoming permanent. At the same time, Spain is under significant fiscal pressure, making it important that measures are cost effective. Faced with this dilemma, it is key to:

- Implement reforms to address remaining structural impediments for firms to create jobs and improve competitiveness, notably as concerns employment protection and wage bargaining.

- Improve activation of the unemployed, by reforming placement services and scaling up of effective and well-targeted active labour market policies, especially for young workers.

- Improve relevant skills, notably for young people, by widening access to upper secondary education.

In February 2012, the government introduced a package of wide-ranging labour market measures. The measures took immediate effect by decree; the law has been in force since July 2012. In general, these reforms are a substantial step in the right direction. While it is still too early to assess the impact of the reform, there are areas where they need to be complemented so as to address these challenges, as described below.

Ensuring that employment protection is not a burden for hiring

Reform of employment protection legislation is key to reducing disincentives of firms to hire on permanent contracts. High dismissal costs on permanent contracts, as compared to temporary contracts, makes firms reluctant to convert temporary contracts into permanent ones, leading to a dual labour market (OECD, 2010a). High protection of workers on permanent contracts also reduces the responsiveness of wages to labour market conditions and makes the integration of young people into the labour market more difficult. Finally, it harms labour productivity by reducing the occupational mobility of workers with permanent contracts and the incentives of individuals and firms to invest in training on temporary jobs (Mora-Sanguinetti and Fuentes, 2012).

The 2012 labour market reforms aim at reducing duality. If a dismissal is judged unjustified, the maximum compensation is reduced to 33 days' wages per year of seniority (up to a maximum of 24 months), compared with 45 days (and a maximum of 42 months before). This applies to all new contracts and for future years of service on existing contracts. Justified dismissal carries severance pay of only 20 days' wages per year of seniority. A potentially important part of the reform is clarifying what justified dismissal means, as clarity will make it easier to use. This should help bring the reference down to 20 days wages per year of seniority. Firms no longer have to pay interim wages while judicial procedures are pending and collective dismissals have been made easier by doing away with the requirement of approval by a regional or the central government. All in all, employees have less incentive to go to court to claim that the dismissal would have been unjustified.

Under the new law, dismissal can be judged justified for economic reasons if the company faces a decline in revenues over three consecutive quarters as compared to the previous year. The possibility to shed labour in bad times should raise the incentive of firms to use permanent contracts and it should improve wage flexibility. In good times the reform should also facilitate restructuring and flexibility, but it remains to be seen how many dismissals will be judged as justified by the courts. In any case, severance pay for unjustified dismissal should be further reduced, as even at 33 days' wages, firing costs for unfair dismissals remain high in international comparison. In particular, the difference with respect to firing costs of workers on temporary contracts remains large. If the reform does not prove effective in reducing duality substantially, moving to a single contract with initially low but gradually increasing severance payments could reduce the difference in dismissal costs of temporary and permanent contracts.

The 2012 reforms reinstate the limit of 24 months on the duration of fixed-term contracts, but this limit had little effect in the past. It can be circumvented by redefining the job and rehiring the same workers on another temporary contract after an unemployment spell. In the medium term, making employers' contributions to the unemployment insurance fund depend on the firm's dismissal history – such as the experience-rating of the unemployment insurance in the United States – could help reduce this risk and help reduce duality. It would, however, imply a *de facto* increase in employment protection, highlighting the need to revisit policy in this area.

Promoting job creation through more flexible adjustment of wages

Reform of collective bargaining is especially important to promote job creation through more flexible adjustment of wages and hours worked, thereby improving competitiveness. In Spain firms had limited leeway in adjusting working conditions to external or internal conditions, as reflected in collectively bargained wages that were increasing even in a situation of very high unemployment (Figure 7). This is due to a complex system of collective bargaining, predominantly at the sectoral or regional level, and the extension of such bargains by law to all firms of the same sector or region, even if they were not represented in the negotiations.

Figure 7. **Wage costs**
Per cent growth

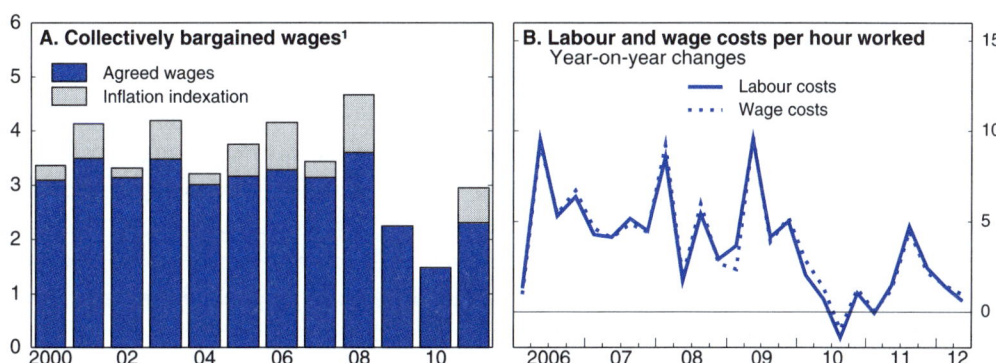

1. Data for 2010 and 2011 are provisional.
Source: Ministerio de Empleo y Seguridad Social (2012), *Boletín de Estadísticas Laborales*; and Banco de España (2012), *Indicadores Económicos Database*, November.

StatLink ⟐ *http://dx.doi.org/10.1787/888932740309*

The 2012 labour market reforms allow companies to reach firm-level collective agreements, removing the restrictions sector-level bargaining could impose on such agreements. Firms can more easily opt-out from collective agreements if employers and workers fail to agree; in this case, the reform introduced binding arbitration. Firms can unilaterally alter employment contracts. Finally, the reform limits to one year the maximum time period during which the conditions of a collective agreement remain in force beyond the period originally foreseen in the agreement.

These steps significantly improve flexibility of work conditions at the firm level, which is welcome. Nevertheless, some collective wage agreements may still apply up to 4 years as some are negotiated for 3 years and could be in force for another year following the foreseen end period. This could make wages less responsive to economic conditions, although the measures described above improve flexibility and nominal wage growth per worker fell to 0% in the second quarter. For firms failing to reach a firm-level agreement, legal extension will require them to apply higher-level agreements. The outcomes of new firm-level agreements are likely to remain conditioned by legally extended sectoral agreements, as these will in most cases provide the fall-back option if a firm-level agreement is not reached. However, high-level agreements may also become more flexible to changes in economic conditions in response to the implemented reforms. Moreover, individual firms cannot decide whether to participate in sectoral wage negotiations or not. Another option to avoid these drawbacks is to abolish legal extension and replace it by an opt-in system, where employers decide whether to be represented in sectoral wage bargaining.

Strengthening activation

Increasing job-search assistance for young people experiencing difficulties in finding a job has proven effective in other countries and is especially needed in Spain, in the light of the large share of young people who are neither in employment nor in education or training (OECD, 2010b). Also, in a recession, the lower opportunity cost of time spent on training makes it an especially opportune timing to increase them. Training would also help the unemployed acquire a different set of skills so as to prepare for a job outside their previous occupation. This is particularly important for Spain where the economic recovery requires significant structural change. The government is designing measures to address these issues.

While unemployment insurance has so far helped limit the social costs of the economic and financial crisis, rising long-term unemployment has lowered the coverage of unemployment insurance as benefits are being exhausted. Hence, effective placement services and activation of the unemployed are critical to lowering unemployment and avoiding it from becoming permanent. The 2012 reform authorises temporary employment agencies to act as placement agencies. This is welcome. However, requirements for benefit recipients to engage in active job search activities need to be better enforced, although some steps have been taken to make progress. The division of responsibilities may distort placement incentives for regional employment offices as regions do not receive the fiscal benefits of a reduction in unemployment. Comprehensive monitoring and evaluation of placement services and ALMP implementation at regional level, based on quantitative output indicators, help to improve incentives for regional employment services (OECD 2008, 2010a). Some steps are being taken in this direction.

While a wide range of hiring subsidies have been abolished in 2012, new subsidies were introduced for the hiring of vulnerable groups, including young people, by firms with fewer than 50 employees. The 2012 reform has scaled up subsidies for firms hiring workers on permanent contracts. The experience from previous downturns has shown that under conditions of very weak labour demand such incentives can jump-start job creation, in particular if targeted at vulnerable groups (OECD, 2010c). However, these subsidies should only be used as a temporary instrument while activity remains weak, and they should be applied only to most disadvantaged youth. Subsidies to private-sector employment otherwise have large dead-weight and substitution effects, which may increase with the recovery (De Serres *et al.*, 2010). Hence, as labour markets tighten, most schemes will ultimately yield little in terms of net employment gains, but will be costly for public finances. This indeed was the experience in Spain in periods of economic expansion (OECD, 2010a).

Ensuring that youth acquire the skills needed in the labour market

The share of the low-skilled among all young unemployed has been particularly high in Spain in international comparison and has increased drastically since 2007, reflecting weaknesses in the education system and a poor school to work transition. Policy makers should encourage youth to stay in formal or vocational education to boost their skills and longer term employability. Two priorities stand out: reducing the high drop-out rate and improving vocational education.

The graduation rate from lower secondary education has been very low and has barely increased during the crisis, reaching only 75% in 2010. Relatively strict requirements to pass compulsory (lower) secondary education have contributed to frequent grade repetition and eventual high drop out from compulsory education. Besides the adverse effects on employability of the student, grade repetition creates large costs for the society as a whole. The government should narrow criteria for granting pupils' promotion to subsequent grades, and hence access to upper secondary education, on those core competencies that are instrumental for following any type of upper secondary education. At the same time, efforts should continue to raise educational outcomes.

Improved vocational education is needed to provide youth at risk of dropping out with work-related skills and an alternative option to attain upper secondary education. In Spain, the incentives for young people to follow vocational streams have been weak, as reflected in relatively low graduation rates from vocational programmes. Moreover, the skills acquired do not match those asked for in the labour market (OECD, 2008), linked to the limited participation of businesses in school-based programmes. An alternative option to acquire practical skills, the training contract, has proven unattractive, too. The skills acquired through these contracts have not been formally recognised, making young people reluctant to take on such jobs (OECD, 2007). Training contracts have also been typically too short for firms to draw a net return from the investment in the training.

The government envisages improving school-based vocational education and the training contracts. These two elements should be combined within a single scheme, the period for which training contracts are signed extended, and work-based training provided through training contracts alternated with school-based training. These reforms would raise the attractiveness of vocational training for both young people and firms: students would receive a wage and the contents of work-based and school-based training would be more closely linked. By paying wages, firms would participate in the financing of the system, and are expected to be willing to do so because they receive benefits in terms of access to a better workforce. The government should concentrate mainly on the provision of the school-based part of the training, increasing spending efficiency.

Box 4. **Key recommendations on labour market reform**

- Further reduce compensation for unjustified dismissal. If the reform does not prove effective in reducing duality substantially, a single contract with initially low but gradually increasing severance payments would help reduce the still large difference in dismissal costs between temporary and permanent contracts. This would reduce duality effectively.

- An option to improve the flexibility to react to economic conditions, is to abolish legal extension of higher level collective bargaining agreements or replace it by an opt-in system, where employers decide whether to be represented in sectoral wage bargaining.

- Extend access to training and job-search assistance for unemployed youth. Introduce comprehensive monitoring and benchmarking of placement services and ALMP implementation at regional level.

- Widen access to upper secondary education by narrowing criteria for grade advancement in lower secondary education to core competencies. Combine the school-based vocational education system and training contracts into one single scheme.

Reforms to raise productivity can strengthen competitiveness

Structural estimates based on the 2008 sectoral PMR indicators suggest that aligning product market regulation in network and services sectors with international best practice could raise the level of labour productivity in Spain by up to 7% over ten years (Arnold *et al.*, 2009). Were Spain to adopt best-practice regulation in sectors that are important providers of intermediate inputs to the economy, average annual MFP growth could be around 1.6 percentage points higher for the manufacturing sector and 0.8 percentage points for the whole economy over a 5-year period (Bourlès *et al.*, 2011). Both results assume best practice in each single sector and quick phasing-in.

The Spanish economy has experienced significantly weaker labour productivity growth than other OECD economies since the mid-1990s. In recent years labour productivity growth has accelerated, but this recovery is likely to have been due to cyclical and to other temporary factors related to the destruction of low-productivity temporary jobs, notably in the construction sector (Mora-Sanguinetti and Fuentes, 2012). Total factor productivity growth has been low across a wide range of sectors (Mora-Sanguinetti and Fuentes, 2012), suggesting that broad-based policy action could strengthen performance. Labour market reforms have an important role to play in raising productivity performance.

Empirical evidence suggests that part of the weak productivity performance is related to relatively low firm turnover and the large size of a relatively low-productivity small business sector (Mora-Sanguinetti and Fuentes, 2012). This evidence indicates that the barriers to entry and to firm growth hold back advances in productivity. Onerous regulation of employment relationships can raise the cost of employment, relative to self-employment, and would, therefore, be expected to create barriers for successful firms to grow. Growth of successful firms is a key driving force of output and productivity growth (*e.g.* Wong and Autio, 2005, and references therein).

OECD product market regulation indicators show that the administrative costs of creating a business are relatively high. Moreover, licensing requirements on large retail surface outlets remain onerous. Some entry barriers in the professional services also appear unnecessary, as qualification requirements are more stringent than in other EU countries. Entry barriers to road transport could also be reduced further (Annex A1). While recent reform has reduced the costs of creating a business, the number of procedures necessary to register a business is still relatively high as compared to other countries. The government has raised the minimum number of weekly hours that regional governments must allow retailers to be open (regions are free to allow more extensive opening hours, but not more restrictive ones). This limit, which is now quite low, should be raised substantially beyond what is currently planned. The government should also eliminate restrictions on pricing below cost. The government also aims to limit the range of activities which are restricted to specific professional groups and to eliminate barriers that are deemed unjustified for the access and exercise of professional services. All these measures are welcome. In addition, the costs of creating businesses should be reduced and sector-specific entry barriers eliminated, including for professional services as well as road transport.

Policies to ensure sustainable and efficient use of natural resources are critical to ensure sustainable expansion of activity. Water policies are particularly important in Spain, as scarcity is marked and water resources are used intensively. As recommended in the previous *OECD Economic Survey of Spain* water prices will need to rise further so as to reflect costs in full. Higher revenues from improved cost recovery would generate private funding for investment, providing near-term economic stimulus. Further steps need to be taken to halt excessive groundwater abstractions. Risks of regulatory capture of regulatory authorities by large water consumers should be reduced by widening the participatory approach to a wider set of stakeholders, such as scientists or representatives of institutions protecting local ecosystems. Benchmark regulation of water utilities would contribute to more efficient water supply and treatment services.

Box 5. **Key recommendations on product market reform**

- Further reduce the costs and procedures necessary to create businesses and eliminate sector-specific entry barriers, including for professional services as well as rail and road transport.

- Entry barriers for large-surface retail outlets imposed by regional governments should be lowered, and shop opening hours should be liberalised in those regions where restrictions remain. Raise the minimum opening hours regional governments have to apply.

Bibliography

Allard, C. and L. Everaert (2010), "Lifting Euro Area Growth: Priorities for Structural Reforms and Governance", *IMF Staff Position Note*, 22 November.

Ahrend, R., J. Arnold and C. Moeser (2011), "The Sharing of Macroeconomic Risk", *OECD Economics Department Working Papers*, No. 877, OECD Publishing.

Arnold, J., P. Höller, M. Morgan and A. Wörgötter (2009), "Structural Reforms and the Benefits of the Enlarged EU Internal Market: Much Achieved and Much to Do", *OECD Economics Department Working Papers*, No. 694.

Bouis, R., B. Cournède and A.K. Christensen (2012), "Implications of Output Gap Uncertainty in Times of Crisis", *OECD Economics Department Working Papers*, No. 977.

Bouis, R. and R. Duval (2011), "Raising Potential Growth after the Crisis: A Quantitative Assessment of the Potential Gains from Various Structural Reforms in the OECD Area and Beyond", *OECD Economics Department Working Papers*, No. 835.

Bourlès, R., G. Cette, J. Lopez, J. Mairesse and G. Nicoletti (2010), "Do Product Market Regulations in Upstream Sectors Curb Productivity Growth? Panel Data Evidence for OECD Countries", *OECD Economics Department Working Papers*, No. 791.

De Serres, A., F. Murtin, C. de la Maisonneuve (2012), "Tackling Unemployment in a Weak Post-Crisis Recovery: Policies to Facilitate the Return to Work", forthcoming as *OECD Economics Department Working Papers*, OECD Publishing.

Financial Stability Board (FSB) (2011), "Key Attributes of Effective Resolution Regimes for Financial Institutions".

Hagemann, R. (2012), "Fiscal Consolidation: Part 6. What Are the Best Policy Instruments for Fiscal Consolidation?", *OECD Economics Department Working Papers*, No. 937, OECD Publishing.

International Monetary Fund (IMF) (2002), *Building Strong Banks Through Surveillance and Resolution*, Washington, DC.

IMF (2012a), "Financial Sector Stability Assessment", Washington, DC.

IMF (2012b), "From Bail-out to Bail-in: Mandatory Debt Restructuring of Systemic Financial Institution", *IMF Staff Discussion Note*, April, Washington, DC.

Joumard, I., P. Höller, C. André and C. Nicq (2010), *Health Care Systems: Efficiency and Policy Settings*, OECD Publishing.

Joumard, I., M. Pisu and D. Bloch (2012), "Less Income Inequality and More Growth – Are They Compatible? Part 3. Income Redistribution via Taxes and Transfers Across OECD Countries", *OECD Economics Department Working Papers*, No. 926, OECD Publishing.

Ministerio de Economía y Competitividad (2012), "Update of the Stability Programme".

Ministerio de Economía y Hacienda (MEH, 2011), "Reform of the Spanish Pension System", *www.thespanisheconomy.com/SiteCollectionDocuments/en-gb/Economic%20Policy%20Measures/110627%20Spanish%20Pensions%20System%20Reform.pdf*.

Ministry of Labour and Social Security (2012), *Bulletin of Labour Market Statistics*.

Mora-Sanguinetti, J.S. and A. Fuentes (2012), "An Analysis of Productivity Performance in Spain Before and During the Crisis: Exploring the Role of Institutions", *OECD Economics Department Working Papers*, No. 973, OECD Publishing.

OECD (2006), *OECD Employment Outlook*, Paris.

OECD (2007), *Jobs for Youth: Spain*, Paris.

OECD (2008), *OECD Economic Surveys: Spain*, Paris.

OECD (2010a), *OECD Economic Surveys: Spain*, Paris.

OECD (2010b), *Off to a Good Start? Jobs for Youth*, Paris.

OECD (2010c), *OECD Employment Outlook*, Paris.

OECD (2011a), *OECD Economic Surveys: European Union*, Paris.

OECD (2011b), *OECD Economic Surveys: Euro Area*, Paris.

Schich, S. and B.H. Kim (2012), "Developments in the value of implicit guarantees for bank debt: The role of resolution regimes and practices", forthcoming in *OECD Journal: Financial Market Trends*.

Schich, S. and S. Lindh (2012), "Implicit Guarantees for Bank Debt: Where Do We Stand?", *OECD Journal: Financial Market Trends*, Vol. 2012, Issue 1.

ANNEX A1

Progress in main structural reforms

This table reviews action taken on recommendations from previous *Surveys*. Recommendations that are new in this *Survey* are listed at the end of the relevant chapter.

Recommendations in previous *Survey*	Action taken since December 2010
Improve Fiscal Policy across levels of government	
Budget outcomes of regional governments should be published in a timely manner.	Since 2012 quarterly data on national accounting basis are published for Autonomous Communities. First quarter data were published in June, complementing the quarterly releases on a cash-basis. Legislation has been passed requiring the provision of monthly data on cash and national accounts basis for Autonomous Communities and on a quarterly basis for municipalities. The first monthly release on a cash basis was published in October.
Ensure that the budgetary rules across levels of government require substantial surpluses in periods in which economic activity is above the national potential. Rules concerning budget balances for the regional governments could be set as a function of the national output gap, rather than growth rates of output.	The new Organic Law on Budgetary Stability and Financial Sustainability requires all jurisdictions of general government to be at least in structural balance from 2020 onwards, taking into account the national output gap.
Make stronger use of benchmarking of regional government services with respect to quality and cost of services they provide. For instance, link transfers to poor regions to education outcomes, such as graduation rates in upper secondary vocational education.	Benchmarking of local governments is envisaged in the draft Law for Rationalisation and Sustainability of Local Administration to evaluate efficiency of expenditure and quality of services.
Grant the public policy evaluation agency a high degree of independence from the political process and ensure its findings are easily available to the general public.	The draft Transparency Act sets up a Transparency Agency, replacing the public policy evaluation agency. The appointment of its president will have to be accepted by a parliamentary committee. All assessments reports are published on the website.
Reduce ageing cost and improve fiscal sustainability	
Implement the increase in the legal retirement age from 65 to 67 years and begin indexing the statutory retirement age to changes in life expectancy.	The legal retirement age will rise gradually to 67 years from 2013 to 2027 for workers with contribution records of less than 38.5 years. An indexation mechanism has not been defined but a legal obligation exists to introduce one by 2027 at the latest and may be introduced earlier if the pension system is in deficit.
Base pension entitlements on a participant's lifetime earnings rather than the final 15 years.	The assessment base will rise to 25 years from 2013 to 2022.
Reduce the average annual accrual rate sufficiently to lengthen the duration of the contribution record needed to obtain a full pension.	The number of contribution years to qualify for the full pension gradually increases from 35 to 37 years, from 2013 to 2027 and the accrual rates are adjusted accordingly.
Reduce the duration and gradually phase out supplementary unemployment benefits paid to older workers until they reach retirement. Consider increasing the "bonus" for postponing retirement beyond the statutory retirement age. Abolish subsidies for partial retirement.	The age for receiving the unemployment benefits for older workers has been raised from 52 to 55 years. Discount and bonus payments for retirement before and after the legal age, respectively, were raised. Subsidies for partial retirement were removed, but partial early retirement is not subject to discounts.

Recommendations in previous *Survey*	Action taken since December 2010
Continue tightening eligibility for survivors' pensions through closer scrutiny of employability of beneficiaries. Phase out benefits to non-immediate family beneficiaries, and integrate survivor benefits more closely with own old-age pension benefits.	None.
Phase out special schemes and integrate them into the general public pension system. Introduce discounts for pensions of all civil servants retiring before the legal retirement age.	The special regimes for civil servants has been abolished for new workers. The special regimes for agricultural workers and for workers in households has been abolished for all workers.

Make the tax system more growth friendly

Consider shifting some of the burden of labour taxes to consumption taxes, e.g. by reducing the use of preferential value added tax rates.	The standard VAT rate was raised by 3 percentage points and the reduced rate by 2 in 2012. Some goods and services were moved from the lower to the standard rate. Increases of environmental taxes are planned.
Consider reducing taxation of corporations. Phase out preferential rates for small businesses.	None.
Improve local government's reliance on real estate tax and abolish the local business tax. Lower taxes on housing transactions.	Real estate taxes were raised temporarily in 2012 and 2013 nation-wide. Tax subsidies for the refurbishment of private homes will be eliminated in 2013.

Improve the functioning of the housing market

Eliminate or further reduce remaining tax subsidies for housing and for rental properties. Replace them with a means-tested cash benefit for low-income households, earmarked to rent payments.	Tax deduction in house mortgages will be removed for purchases as from 2013.

Improving the functioning of the labour market

Further ease the burden on businesses to prove that dismissals are justified. Steps to reduce the duration of judicial procedures would also help.	The labour market reform legislated in July 2012 eases the burden on businesses to prove that dismissals are justified and reforms the judicial procedures for dismissals (Chapter 2). The administrative authorisation for collective dismissals has been eliminated.
Consider the introduction of a single work contract with gradually increasing severance payments according to length of service.	Unfair dismissal compensation was reduced and causes for fair dismissal were clarified. A new contract with a one-year probationary period, during which no dismissal compensation rights accrue, was introduced for firms with fewer than 50 employees (see Chapter 2).
Ensure that firms and workers can freely agree to opt out of higher level collective agreements.	Implemented.
Consider abolishing the statutory extension principle. Or replace it with an opt-in system that allows employers the choice of whether to adopt the agreement.	The period of validity of collective agreements beyond their expiry date if renegotiation fails was reduced to one year and prevalence was given to firm level agreements.
Encourage the elimination of inflation indexation clauses in collective bargaining.	The social partners' agreement of January 2012 encourages fixing wages according to productivity.
Redirect subsidies for hiring unemployed on permanent contracts to better targeted active labour market programmes (ALMPs).	Most subsidies have been eliminated except those for young workers at SMEs and for people with disabilities.
Provide the most disadvantaged youth access to closely monitored early activation and job-search assistance programmes.	It is planned to focus a gradual reform of ALMPs on youth.
Ideally, the responsibilities for funding of unemployment benefits and for managing the public employment services should be assigned to the same jurisdictional level (the central government). At least, introduce comprehensive monitoring and evaluation of employment services at the regional level, based on quantitative output indicators or targets. Successful regional placement services should receive a financial reward.	A new co-ordination scheme is in force. Regional employment services will be monitored and funds distributed in part according to performance. Evaluation mechanisms are planned.
Do not pay benefit payment retrospectively for the period prior to registration and make the first full interview mandatory at the time of registration. Increase the frequency of reporting of job search activity. Consider reducing the duration of unemployment benefit entitlements.	The unemployment benefit has been reduced for workers who have been unemployed for more than six months. Conditions for receiving the benefit have been strengthened.

Recommendations in previous *Survey*	Action taken since December 2010
Improving the integration of immigrants	
Improve the recognition of foreign qualifications through bilateral agreements with originating countries and an on-the-job skill assessment programme.	The central government has transferred funds to the autonomous communities to facilitate the recognition of professional competences acquired through work.
Improve public language training. Adapt the national system of language certification to the needs of the labour market.	None.
Allow non EU immigrants (with a valid permit) to hold jobs in at least some parts of the public administration.	None.
Further improving access to and quality of early childhood education	
Disburse central government subsidies for accredited childcare facilities in the form of vouchers to low income households with children, covering the full cost of a place in accredited childcare.	The central government plans to offer funding to regional governments in 2013, yet to widen public provision for 0-2 year-old children, although the available amount is not decided.
Raising the share of students graduating from upper secondary education	
Enforce the prohibition of raising fees from parents in publicly funded primary and lower secondary schools as well as of selection criteria. Ensure a level playing field in the rules assigning resources to public and publicly funded private schools.	None.
Link the disbursement of subsidies to upper secondary schools to the obligation of offering schooling free of charge.	None.
Widen the choice of options at the final stage of compulsory schooling and focus the conditions for granting pupils promotion to subsequent grades and access to upper secondary education more narrowly on those core competencies that are needed to follow any type of upper secondary education.	The government intends to undertake a review of all Secondary Education. It will open the choice of options at the final stage of compulsory schooling and focus teaching more strongly on core competencies.
Raise child benefits and make them conditional on continued attendance in full time education.	None.
Extend external testing at the school level to all regions, and use this to benchmark performance against targets.	National external testing and assessment for primary and secondary education are undergoing a review processes.
Widen autonomy of schools, notably with respect to hiring decisions of teaching staff and curricular content and give schools powers to hire, reward and dismiss teachers.	Steps are planned in the new Law of Education.
Strengthen higher education	
Publish the results of the national quality assurance agencies' assessments on a regular and comprehensive basis.	All the quality assurance agencies for higher education publish the evaluation reports on all programmes offered by universities on the web. These reports contain suggestions for improvement which are later monitored.
Remove the obstacles to university teachers moving to the private sector and participating in spin-off firms. Increase the freedom of universities to recruit non-permanent professors and to adjust all professors' remuneration according to performance.	The Science, Technology and Innovation Bill in force since 2011 provides a legal framework for collaborative research projects (including intellectual property rights). It promotes the sharing of technology between teaching and research on one side, and businesses on the other.
Introduce loans with income contingent repayments for all tertiary education students. Increase fees at public universities and introduce fees for tertiary vocational courses.	No action on loans since the introduction of interest-free loans for master's degree courses in 2007. Fees were raised in many universities in 2012.
Link university funding more strongly to indicators of teaching output. Strengthen further the independence of universities, notably with regard to the setting of contract conditions and pay.	None.
Raising the attractiveness of vocational and continuous education	
Open up the teaching profession in vocational schools more widely to practitioners.	A pilot programme launched for 3 years in 2012 facilitates knowledge transfer between schools and enterprises and will be evaluated. Legislation is being prepared to regulate apprenticeship contracts and dual VET.

Recommendations in previous *Survey*	Action taken since December 2010
Make the system of continuous training less complicated and less stringent and facilitate the access of small firms. Improve the options of firms as to the choice of training in order to ensure that it meets the actual training needs of the firms.	The labour reform has introduced competition in the selection of providers and centralised priorities with the Employment annual Plan. Training contracts have been reformed (see Chapter 2).
Introduce training vouchers to individual adults covering course fees and indirect costs such as foregone wages. Guarantee provider quality by ensuring that accredited training providers meet strict quality standards.	The labour reform introduces a voucher (cuenta formacion) that still needs to be developed.

Improving the functioning of product markets

Increase the independence of sectoral regulatory bodies and strengthen their powers.	The independence of sector regulators was strengthened in 2011. From 2012 a new multisector supervision authority, the Comisión Nacional de los Mercados y la Competencia (CNMC) a will enforce competition policy and supervise telecoms, transport and energy, replacing the competition commission and the sector regulators. The new authority will have full independence from public and private entities. The appointment of the counsellors will be ratified by Parliament with a fixed, non-renewable mandate of six years. However, the board members of the disappearing independent regulators will be removed before their term ends. In telecommunications, some competencies will be moved to the government.
Further reduce barriers to the establishment of new firms.	In 2010 and 2011 several initiatives were implemented to facilitate the creation of businesses including shortening procedures to create limited liability companies to between 1 and 5 days. Local licensing are required to be abolished except for well-defined exceptions. The use of electronic systems was fostered to reduce the cost and time taken to create a business. Limits on the duration and cost of the notary and the registry procedures were imposed. In 2012 local license requirement schemes for shops and other consumer services with a surface of less than 300 m^2 were eliminated.
Reduce the regulatory obstacles to institutional investors' participation in venture-capital companies.	None.

Energy markets

Reform the current system of energy generation capacity payments by providing a variable payment that is linked to the use of capacity.	The regulatory authority is working on a proposal. Some regulated payments for distribution, transport, availability of generation capacity, insular generation and other were cut.
Phase out regulated retail gas and electricity prices.	Regulated retail tariffs were raised by 7% in 2012.

Post and telecommunications

Give the telecom regulator responsibility for consumer protection.	None.
Allow the regulator, in an explicit manner, to mandate the functional separation of the incumbent as a measure of last resort.	None. The government takes such decisions on the basis of information received by the regulator.
Ensure an appropriate level of access of competitors to the public postal network and ensure access to the address databases of the postal services incumbent.	None.

Transport services

Make the tender of regional passenger rail transport services compulsory. Require the incumbent to make its rolling stock available with non discriminating conditions.	Implemented by the end of 2012. Passenger rail services will be fully opened to market entrants in 2013. The incumbent operator has been split into 4 companies.
Remove the constraints involved in obtaining a road freight haulage operating license and reform the authorisation process to make consolidation of firms easier. Ensure that road passenger transport licenses are tendered on a competitive basis without favouring incumbents.	A modification of road transport legislation is planned to harmonise it with EU regulation and simplify administrative obligations for operators. It also aims at strengthening competition in services tendered publicly.

Recommendations in previous *Survey*	Action taken since December 2010
Retail trade and professional services	
In retail trade, regional governments should reduce entry restrictions of large retail outlets. Shop opening hours should be liberalised in those regions where restrictions remain. Consider raising the national minimum which applies to the limit that regions can impose when regulating shop opening hours.	The government raised the national minimum on the ceiling regional governments can impose on opening hours from 72 to 90 hours per week and on opening during public holidays from 8 to 10 days. Touristic areas have been defined for which opening hours regime has been fully liberalised.
Amend the excessive and sometimes discriminatory restrictions in the pharmacies sector.	Measures to facilitate entry in the sector are under consideration.
The range of professional services for which Spanish regulation requires specific qualification requirements should be reduced.	A new regulatory framework for professional services is planned aiming at limiting restrictions to those considered necessary and proportional.
Savings banks	
Further reduce the role of regional governments in business decisions of the savings banks. Remove the requirement for regional governments to approve mergers of cajas.	Almost all savings banks have transferred their activity to commercial bank subsidiaries. Some have raised equity from external investors and have been recapitalised by the central government. Reforms have been introduced to their governance (see Chapter 1).
Create independent selection panels supplying a list of possible candidates for management positions in the savings banks.	None.
Reducing greenhouse gas emissions	
Review tax subsidies for energy efficiency. Use the tax system to internalise externalities instead. Consider raising taxes on the use of fossil fuels further and introduce a congestion toll.	Incentives for renewable energy were abolished The government is preparing a draft law on energy market reform. To pay for cumulated deficits between regulated electricity prices and costs a 6% flat tax rate on electricity activity and specific taxes on different sources, including nuclear energy and coal combustion, were introduced.
Support the elimination of the EU rules that allow the sale of only up to 10% of the permits	Implemented.
Review the cost effectiveness of the feed-in tariff regime for renewable electricity sources.	Subsidies have been temporarily stopped for new renewable energy generation plants A review of the Renewable Energy Plan 2011-2020 is foreseen.
Managing water resources efficiently	
Ensure that competencies over water resources that are shared to a significant extent across regions are clearly assigned to the respective river basin authorities and the central government. Ensure a proper co-operation between the different levels of government in the management of water resources.	In 2012 steps were taken to preserve the principle of unity in water management and to promote greater co-ordination. The legislation to transpose of the EU Water Framework Directive in national law ensures administrative co-operation as regards the protection of water resources with the Competent Authority Committees (CACs) created for the river basins involving several autonomous regions.
Reduce risks of regulatory capture of regulatory authorities by large water consumers, by widening the participatory approach in water management to a wider set of stakeholders, notably in river basin authorities. Include scientists and representatives of institutions protecting local ecosystems.	The participation of different stakeholders has been strengthened following the transposition of the Water Framework Directive into domestic law.
Ensure that prices reflect more fully all the costs involved in the provision of water services, including environmental and scarcity costs. Develop methods to determine valuations for the environmental impact of water abstractions. In the short term, ensure that subsidies for irrigation modernisation are conditioned on reductions in the amount of water that is designated in concessions.	None.
Review the method of calculating capital costs and ensure full cost recovery. Consider allowing prices to generate sufficient revenue to fund replacement investment and to fully take into account administration and management costs. Harmonise criteria on the attribution of costs to services with public goods characteristics. Extend water pricing on the basis of volumes consumed, especially in irrigation.	None.

Recommendations in previous *Survey*	Action taken since December 2010
Improve the transparency of the costs of water provision services, making them comparable at the national level. Such data should be used to benchmark costs of service providers. Apply benchmark regulation to prices and quality of service.	Legislation in 2011 has clarified cost-based pricing in some cases, notably in private provision. The government has announced its interest in developing a National Water Plan that contributes to greater administrative co-ordination and greater consistency in water management.
Consider introducing a tax on the consumption of pollutants, for example on nitrogen or on phosphorus. Complement it with specific action programmes for designated areas vulnerable to nitrate contamination and by subsidies to support pollution minimising cultivation, especially in the driest water basins.	None.
Extend water banks to more river basins. Ease restrictions on the trade of water concessions. Introduce regulated third-party access to private infrastructure. Reconsider the requirement not to sell water to users considered to be of lower priority in the law.	None.
Use economic instruments, including tenders or auctions, for the assignment of new water concessions and for the replacement of expiring concessions instead of granting them for free.	None.
Reinforce the monitoring of groundwater abstractions. To this end, endow the river basin authorities with the necessary financial and human resources. Review the sanctioning regime by making it more transparent for water users and by ensuring that sanctions are graded and proportionate to the offence.	Monitoring is being reinforced in line with the provisions of EU law. The rules on penalties have been updated and powers to sanction have been reinforced.
Allow the introduction of a charge for groundwater abstractions to cover the cost of administering and enforcing the groundwater rights and to internalise the common-resource externality.	None.

Chapter 1

Deleveraging the private sector and overcoming the banking crisis

Spain is facing a severe banking crisis, reflecting the bursting of a housing and credit boom, which has resulted in a high debt burden of the private sector and a deep recession. The mutual dependence of the banks' and the government's funding conditions has deepened the crisis, although the planned development of a banking union in the euro area may soften these feedback loops. Deleveraging is progressing, but is likely to weigh on economic growth for several years. Rapid and comprehensive recognition of bank losses is key for restoring confidence in the banking sector and moving towards economic recovery. This requires the rapid resolution of non-viable and the recapitalisation of viable banks with capital needs. The government has taken important steps by tightening the provisioning rules on the banks' real estate exposures. A euro area credit line of up to 100 billion euros will provide funds at favourable terms to capitalise banks, subject to conditions which, when met, will help overcome the banking crisis. Action needs to be taken to force the holders of the substantial hybrid capital and subordinated debt issued by banks to absorb losses, especially when the holders of these instruments are institutional investors. Reform of bankruptcy procedures would help shifting resources from insolvent companies to productive use and could provide more effective relief for those households who have no reasonable prospect of being able to repay their debt.

The financial crisis needs to be addressed quickly

Deleveraging has still a long way to go

Debt in the private-non financial sector is unusually high in international comparison. This is especially true in the business sector (Figure 1.1). Debt-to-GDP ratios have fallen somewhat less from the peak than in the United Kingdom or the United States. Lower nominal GDP growth explains most of the lower decline in debt ratios in Spain whereas net debt reductions are as large or larger (see the analysis in *Banco de España*, 2012a). Changes in the debt stock reflect several factors, including the contribution of debt write-offs and net lending. In Spain, declining net lending explains most debt reduction with write-offs contributing little, especially in the household sector (BdE, 2012a). Low write-offs in the household sector reflect relatively low non-performing-loan ratios on mortgages, which are discussed below. By contrast, in the United States, household debt write-offs appear to have played an important role. This appears to have allowed deleveraging to occur while lending remained relatively strong (see Brown *et al.*, 2012 and BdE, 2012a; although Bhutta, 2012, has a conflicting view).

While debt-write offs can accelerate deleveraging episodes, its role in supporting economic recovery is ambiguous. Defaults aggravate distress among financial intermediaries. Accelerated foreclosure of collateral which accompanies mortgage defaults exacerbates asset price falls, generating a vicious cycle of declining activity and asset prices. In the United States, excessive resort to foreclosure of homes has aggravated hardship among households and generated a vicious cycle of declining asset prices, household consumption and activity (IMF, 2012a). However, writing off debt of creditors who are in any case not in a position to repay is important to restructure the banking sector, maintain sound incentives for prudent lending and reallocate resources to more productive use. It can also limit unnecessary hardship among households (IMF, 2002). The capital misallocation associated with keeping bad loans on the books and refinancing them can depress total factor productivity growth as seems to have occurred in Japan (Cournède and Bouis, 2012). Moreover, investor suspicions that loan losses are not being fully recognised raise risk perceptions and therefore funding costs for the banking sector. Such concerns can generate substantial systemic risks, especially in the context of the euro area debt crisis, with its feedback loops between the health of the banking sector and government finances (OECD, 2011a). Even if potential losses are concentrated in few weak entities, they may affect the Spanish and even the euro area banking system because of financial linkages.

The risks of not recognising bad loans are particularly marked in an environment of low interest rates, policy-induced abundant liquidity and scarce equity capital, as observed at present, because the opportunity cost for a bank of rolling over doubtful loans is low compared with the alternative option of recognising them, especially among weak banks. In the low-interest rate environment of Japan, for example, there is evidence that weakening industries received a disproportionate share of loans, to the detriment of

Figure 1.1. **Debt-GDP ratios of the private non-financial sector across OECD countries**

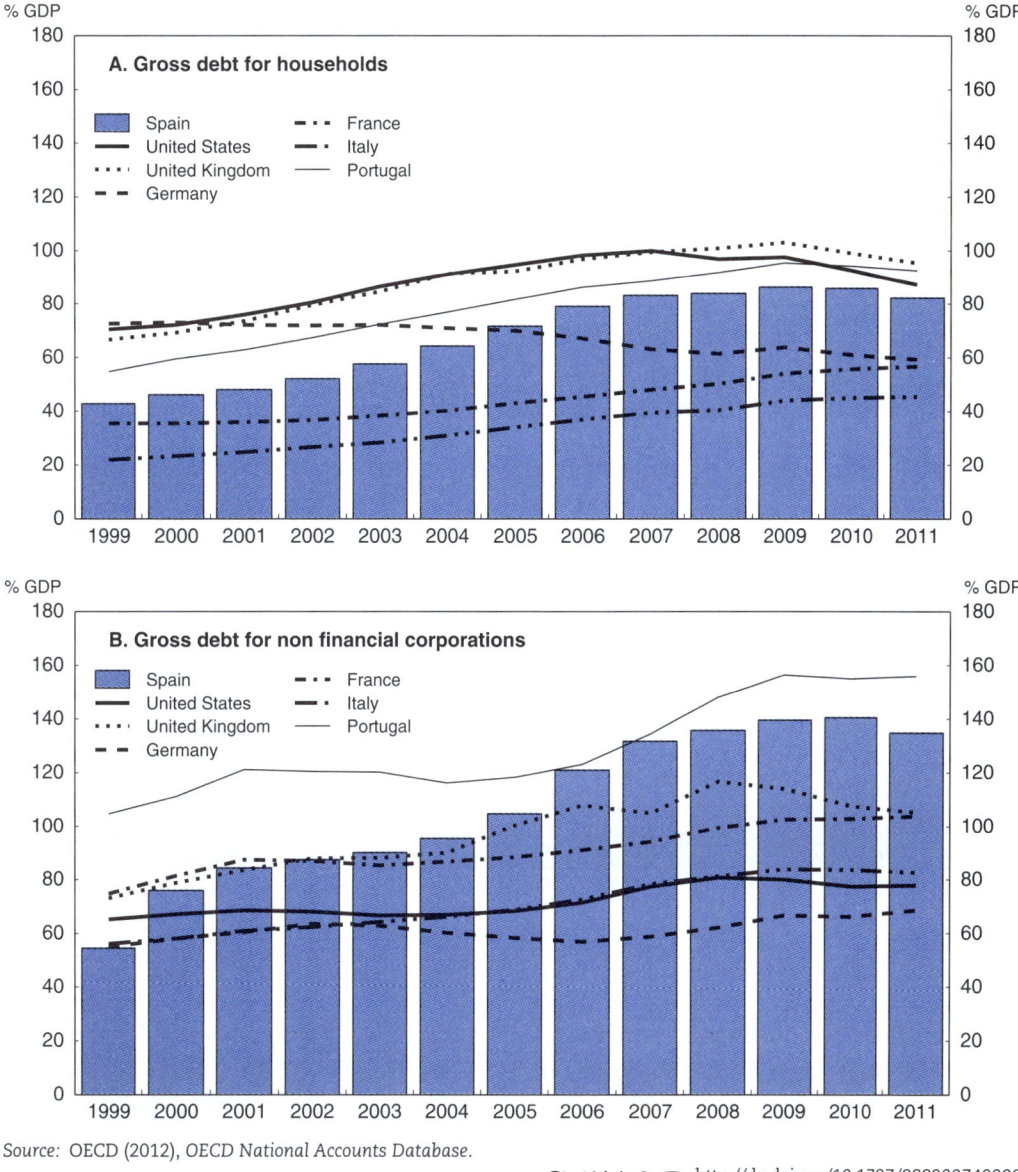

Source: OECD (2012), OECD National Accounts Database.

StatLink ᴍᴤᴸ http://dx.doi.org/10.1787/888932740328

competition and investment by new entrants (Bouis and Cournède and references therein). Recent banking sector reform measures have been taken to address these risks, as discussed below.

Deleveraging episodes are typically particularly long and deep when accompanied by banking and housing crises. Empirical evidence suggests that deleveraging episodes accompanied by a housing crisis took 5 years and a half on average across high-income OECD economies and reduced private debt to GDP ratios by 20 percentage points. If they were accompanied by a banking crisis, they took 7 years, reduced debt to GDP by 30 percentage points on average and were accompanied by a considerably slower recovery in GDP (see *e.g.* Aspachs-Bracons *et al.*, 2011). The evidence presented in IMF (2012a) indicates that housing crises which are preceded by a build-up of household debt result in a fall in real private consumption and GDP of 4%, on average, over a 5 year period. In the absence of a banking crisis the decline in private consumption is limited to 2%.

A factor mitigating deleveraging needs in the current crisis in Spain may be net household wealth. Total net wealth is high relative to disposable income compared to historical averages (Figure 1.2), while net financial wealth is close to historical averages. This may diminish deleveraging needs in the household sector (see also IMF, 2012c). Wealth has been boosted by substantial household saving over the past 15 years, as well as rising house prices until 2007. Household wealth is highly exposed to changes in house prices. While house prices are likely to fall further from current levels, they may, however, not need to return to levels seen before the beginning of the last boom, around 1995 (see below for a discussion of house price developments).

Figure 1.2. **Households' net wealth**

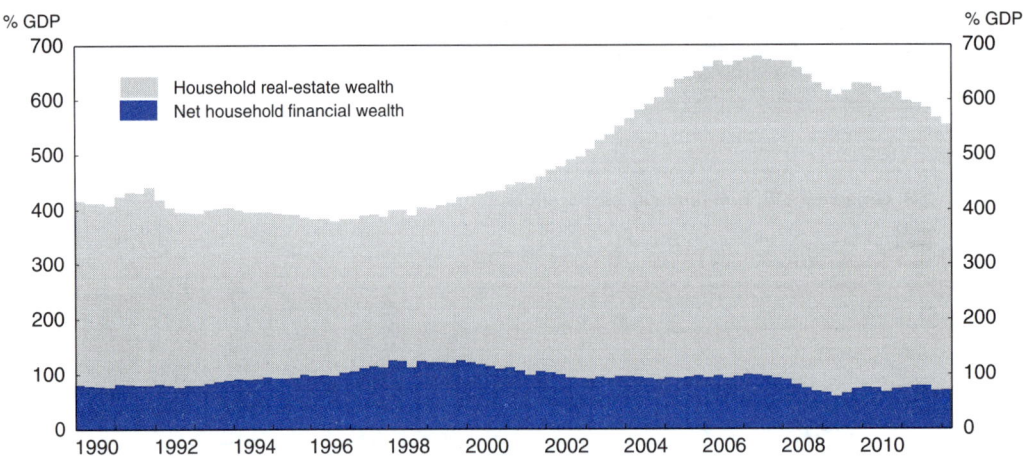

Source: Banco de España (2012), Síntesis de Indicadores, November.

StatLink ⬛ᵍᵖ http://dx.doi.org/10.1787/888932740347

Most debt of non-financial businesses is bank debt. Construction and real estate service companies account for a large share, equivalent to 35% of GDP (Figure 1.3). It is debt in these sectors that accounts for the bulk of differences in business indebtedness in Spain as compared to other European economies (BdE, 2012a, OECD, 2010). Bank loans to construction firms have fallen markedly since 2008. By contrast, loans to the housing development sector continued to rise until 2009 and have fallen modestly since, indicating that progress needs to be made in writing off these loans.

Policy-makers have limited options to support an orderly deleveraging process. The most urgent priority for financial policy is to ensure that bad loans be recognised swiftly, losses be taken, non-viable banks wound down orderly and capital shortfalls be plugged at viable banks (Cournède and Bouis, 2012). Recent measures, discussed below, are pursuing this path. Effective bankruptcy procedures also help to accelerate loan loss recognition and the reallocation of resources to productive use. In some countries, governments have taken measures to restructure household debt, in some cases with the government taking over financial risks (see IMF, 2012a for a description of examples). In view of low non-performing loans and the structure of the mortgage market, there is so far no case for a restructuring

Figure 1.3. **Bank lending to non-financial businesses by sector**

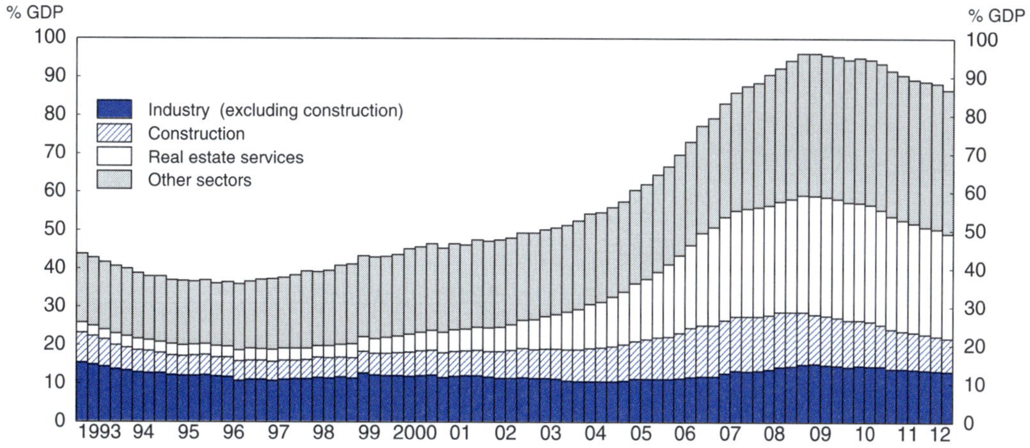

Source: Banco de España (2012), *Síntesis de Indicadores*, August.

StatLink ⟲ http://dx.doi.org/10.1787/888932740366

programme for household mortgage debt in Spain, although there are risks, in part related to a rise in interest rates households pay on their mortgages. In any case, there is limited scope for the government to take on additional financial risks in view of low financial market confidence in government debt and the feedback mechanisms between government debt and the funding costs of banks which characterise the euro area debt crisis. Instead it is necessary to make creditors of bank debt bear losses to limit the impact of the banking crisis on public debt, achieve fairer burden-sharing and protect the taxpayers. These issues are discussed below.

Measures to strengthen potential output growth in the medium term can also help. In Spain, boosting competitiveness and external-demand-driven economic growth is a key element of such a strategy, as all domestic sectors, including the public sector, need to reduce debt burdens. Measures to improve trend productivity growth can strengthen competitiveness while reducing the need to do so via price and wage deflation, which raise the real debt burden.

The housing market is continuing to adjust

House prices have fallen by a cumulated 25% in nominal terms (33% in real terms) since 2008 as of September 2012 (Figure 1.4). This decline is within the range of estimates of the extent of the house price bubble at the peak (see OECD, 2010, for an overview). However, fundamentals, such as household income and unemployment have deteriorated. Hence house prices should be expected to continue falling. This is consistent with developments in housing transactions, which remain weak. Sales of new homes barely exceed completions of housing projects. Hence, the stock of empty housing remains large estimated at around 700 000 (about 3% of the entire housing stock), and is declining only slowly. The share of housing investment in GDP has fallen to less than half of its pre-crisis level and close to historic lows. Housing starts have fallen by 90% and the number of housing units completed has largely converged to the level of housing starts, indicating that the construction of new homes has completed most of its adjustment. Nonetheless, the share of housing investment in GDP remains large in international comparison, which may to some extent be explained by the contribution of tourism to the large stock of holiday homes and related activity in maintenance investment. Tax deductions for refurbishment work also contribute.

Figure 1.4. **The housing market**

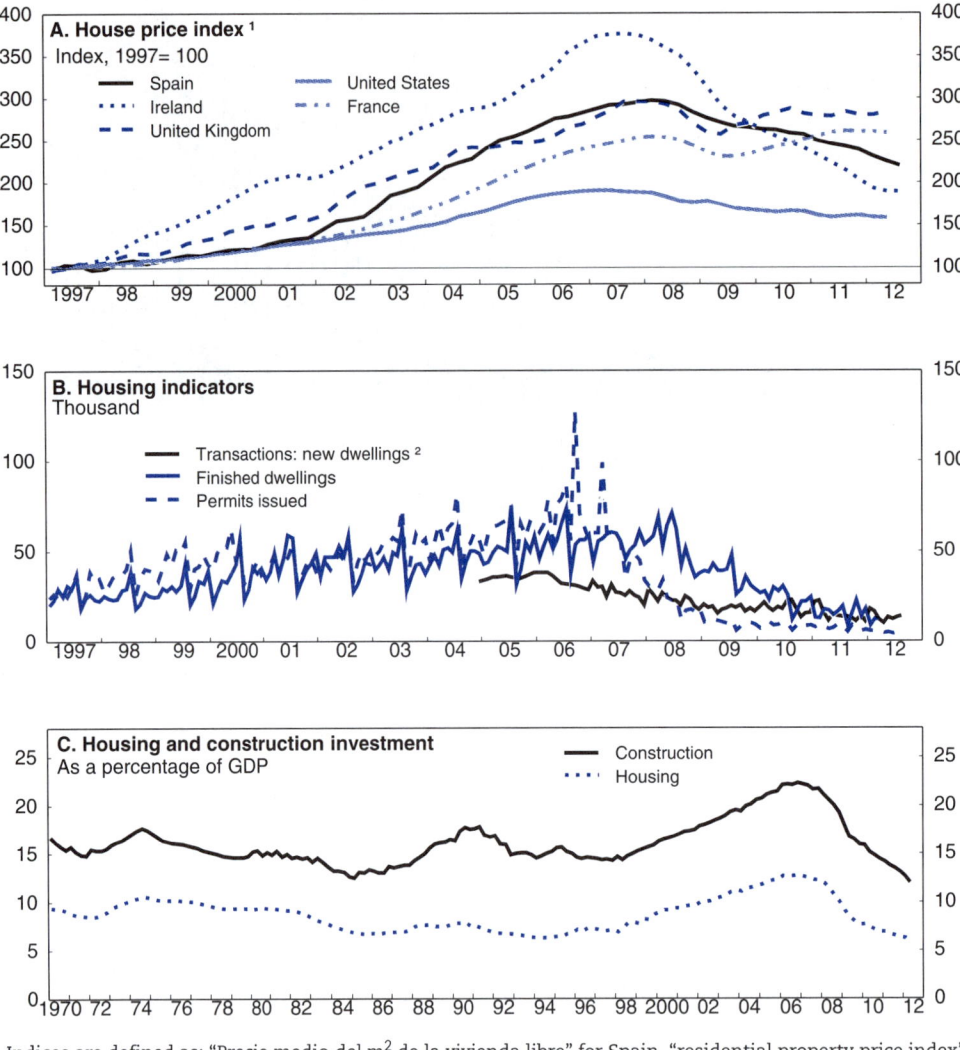

1. Indices are defined as: "Precio medio del m² de la vivienda libre" for Spain, "residential property price index" for Ireland, "mix-adjusted house price index" for United Kingdom, "all transactions index" for the United States, and "indice trimestriel des prix des logements anciens" for France.
2. Registradores.

Source: Banco de España (2012), *Síntesis de Indicadores*, November; and OECD (2012), *OECD Economic Outlook Database*, November.

StatLink ᘓᑒᔆᓓᔆ *http://dx.doi.org/10.1787/888932740385*

A backstop to further falls in house prices may be provided by the fundamentals that have driven part of the rise in demand during the boom, notably rising population and diminishing household size, which may have increased the number of households by 25% since 1998. Employment also rose substantially. These trends have not reversed to a large extent since the onset of the crisis, except with respect to household income (Figure 1.5). Key driving factors behind these developments have been large immigration flows and a large increase in female labour force participation. Since housing supply is not fully elastic on aggregate (being inelastic in densely built metropolitan areas) these are reflected in both prices and quantities. While net immigration flows have turned negative, these driving forces should not be expected to reverse in the future to a large extent, either. However

Figure 1.5. **Developments of some fundamental determinants of housing demand**

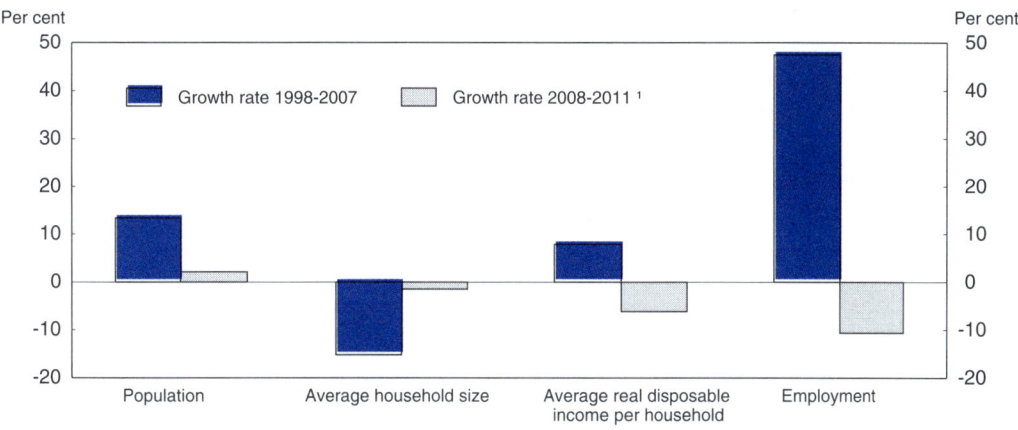

1. 2008-10 for average household size and average real disposable income per household.
Source: INE.

StatLink ᴍꜱᴘ *http://dx.doi.org/10.1787/888932740404*

interest rates are a key determinant of house prices and small variations in interest rates have a large impact on house prices when interest rates are low. While tight mortgage lending conditions are already holding back housing demand, withdrawal of the European Central Bank's (ECB) extraordinary funding facilities could result in substantial increases in interest rates for new mortgages if substantial risk *premia* on the yield of Spanish government bonds persist.

The government has taken some measures to strengthen housing demand

Developing the rented housing market offers some potential for raising the demand for housing and can improve access to adequate housing for low-income households and young individuals, who often cannot afford to buy their home. According to the most recent population census (2001), 11% of households (1.1 million) are housed in physically inadequate conditions or without adequate access to basic services (see *e.g.* FOESSA, 2008). Moreover, 67% of individuals aged between 16 and 35 live in the parental home. This share was similarly high before the rise in youth unemployment and includes young people in employment and full-time higher education. Most housing is owner-occupied. Developing the rented housing market is also important for labour market performance. Rental housing is poorly developed, covering only 13% of the market. Given the existing large housing stock (see above), the government's objective is to promote the rental market as well as the rehabilitation of existing homes and buildings as well as urban environments.

As argued in previous *OECD Economic Surveys* (OECD, 2010) difficulties and delays in the procedures to evict tenants who do not fulfil their contractual obligations have held back the development of the rented housing market, as these difficulties harmed landlords' property rights. Steps to accelerate eviction procedures were taken in 2009. While no comprehensive assessment of the impact of these measures is possible for lack of recent national data on housing tenure status, some evidence points to a significant increase in rental contracts since 2009, although the direct impact of the crisis on households is likely to have played a significant role.[1] The government has taken further measures to accelerate judicial procedures in 2012, doing away with the need of a court case to evict a tenant who does not fulfil contractual obligations, and reducing the period between non-payment of rent and eviction to 10 days. The government also plans to improve judicial resources for the resolution of legal conflicts between landlords and tenants, which is welcome in view of the long duration of court cases. A broader reform of the judiciary is also necessary (Mora and Fuentes, 2012). At the same time, consumer protection concerns need to be safeguarded by avoiding arbitrary evictions and to ensure the existence of a minimum housing safety net, especially at times of economic hardship and in view of the low social assistance benefits paid in Spain. This argument reinforces the case for redirecting housing subsidies to the payment of housing benefits for low-income households, as recommended below. Such benefits could contribute towards a minimum housing safety net.

The regulation of rental contracts was further liberalised in 2012. The initial minimum contract period was reduced from 5 years to 3 years and the first renewal period from 3 years to 1 year. The indexation of rental payments to consumer price inflation within the minimum contract period has been eliminated. The access of owners to their apartment for own needs within the minimum contract periods has been facilitated and landlords can terminate contracts with an advance notice of 2 months, including in the initial period, if the owner or her family need to satisfy own housing needs. However, whether legal regulation of rental prices could have created substantial distortions to the housing market before the reform is uncertain. Rents were by law indexed to consumer price inflation for a period of 5 years (the minimum initial contract period) but could be freely set after the lapse of this period. Therefore, in view of the long economic lifetime of housing, such restrictions are unlikely to distort rental prices significantly. Moreover, contracts could be terminated without further conditions after this initial period and landlords could reserve access to their property for own housing needs within the initial contract period. Barriers to worker mobility have also been reduced by allowing tenants to leave their dwelling with one month's notice before expiration of the contract without paying compensation to the landlord, which is welcome. The effectiveness of these measures in supporting the rented housing market needs to be monitored and followed up if necessary.

Comprehensive tax deductibility of mortgage payments for owner occupiers was reintroduced in 2011 but abolished for new mortgage contracts in 2012 (see OECD, 2007, for a description of the subsidies). The government has also somewhat reduced tax subsidies on existing mortgages. However, taxation of capital gains realised in housing sales has been halved until the end of 2012 and the government has introduced an open-ended reduction of VAT rates for housing purchases from 8 to 4%. Rental income received by home owners also benefits from tax reductions. These tax subsidies introduce distortions, subsidising the housing sector, and are more likely to benefit middle and high-income earners. The government appropriately plans to eliminate the tax subsidies on new mortgage contracts. Further reductions of tax subsidies on existing mortgages may be possible, especially for owners who have already benefited from subsidies for many years and are less likely to face negative equity. Tax advantages for rental income received and capital gains from housing transactions should also be abolished. The budgetary savings could be used to fund a means tested cash benefit earmarked to the housing costs of low income households. Supporting low-income households may also be particularly effective in stabilising domestic demand as their marginal propensity to consume is likely to be relatively high, especially in the context of deleveraging. Further reform of housing taxation should also reduce stamp duties on housing transactions while raising the taxation of real estate property, as recommended in the 2010 *OECD Economic Surveys*. Steps to raise incentives of banks to gradually release housing onto the market would also help to put empty housing stock to good use, helping to reduce housing costs, especially for young households.

The banking crisis requires a comprehensive policy response

Risks in bank balance sheets are concentrated on loans to housing developers

The share of bank loans classified as doubtful has accelerated (Figure 1.6), reaching a level similar to the level attained at the peak following the 1993 recession (BdE, 2012b). About three quarters of loans classified as doubtful are non-performing (see Box 1.1 for the definitions). Doubtful loan ratios have risen particularly sharply among loans to housing developers.

Figure 1.6. **Doubtful loan ratios by sector**
As a percentage of total sectoral loans

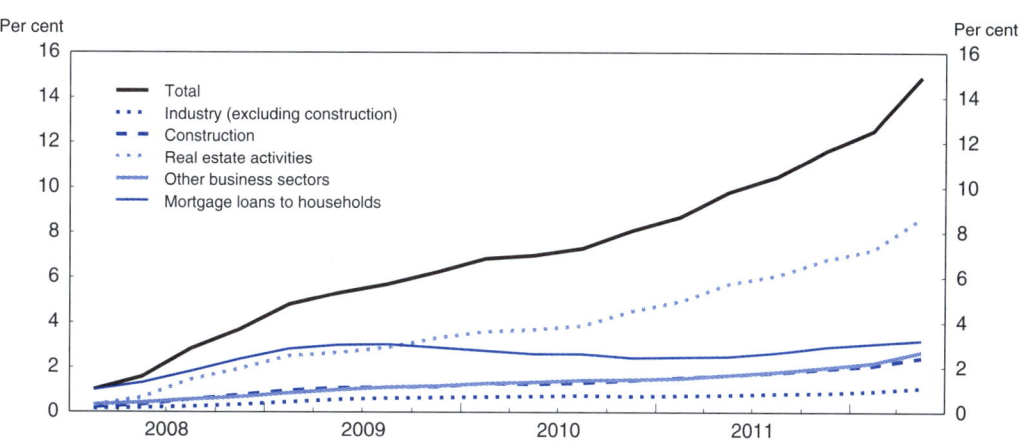

Source: Banco de España(2012), *Boletín Estadístico*, November.

StatLink ᵐˢᵖ *http://dx.doi.org/10.1787/888932740423*

Box 1.1. **Problematic exposures in the balance sheets of Spanish banks**

Non-performing loans: Loans in which some installment has not been paid for a period of more than 90 days.

Doubtful loans: Non-performing loans and loans in which there are reasonable doubts as to total repayment under the terms agreed. For example, inadequate financial structure, negative equity, losses for several years of the debtor automatically lead to classification as doubtful even though the counterparty has not incurred in default or in a delay of payment. Assessments draw on analysis for corporate exposures according to the credit register and assessment of payment delays of debtors to all their creditors.

Substandard loans: Loans showing some general weakness associated with the fact they are to a specific troubled group or sector or if weaknesses are apparent in certain operations weakening their payment ability, even if these operations do not qualify for classification as doubtful or write-off.

Asset foreclosures: Assets which are transferred to banks in exchange for debt extinction.

The total exposure of banks to domestic construction and housing development sectors amounted to about 300 billion euros end-2011 (Figure 1.7), equivalent to 29% of GDP or 9% of consolidated bank balance sheets. This figure excludes loans to firms whose main business is in one of these two sectors but which finance other activities, as some Spanish construction and real estate companies conduct much business in a wide range of activities which are not subject to the risks of the domestic real estate market, in many cases abroad. About two thirds of the exposure belongs to banking groups that originated from savings banks, according to the data published by individual banks. This exceeds their share in total domestic loans to the private sector, which amounts to about 55%.[2] Moreover, since the largest commercial banks are internationally diversified, their domestic loan portfolios weigh much less heavily in their balance sheets. At the end of 2011 banks had provisions worth 6½ per cent of GDP against exposures to housing development and construction on their books. Hence total unprovisioned exposures to domestic construction and real estate activities amounted to 21½ per cent of GDP. Provisioning requirements were strengthened in the course of 2012 (see below).

Figure 1.7. **Housing market exposures**

As per end-2011

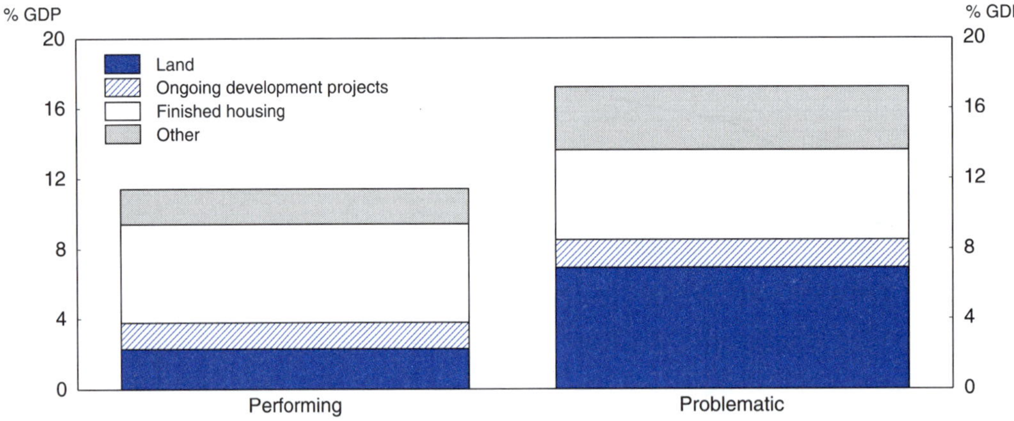

Source: Bank of Spain and Ministry of Economy and Competitiveness.

StatLink ⟪ http://dx.doi.org/10.1787/888932740442

Around 60% of housing development and construction exposures (17% of GDP) were classified as problematic. Among problematic exposures, land stands out with a contribution of more than 70 billion. Loans are classified as problematic before they turn out "non-performing", using forward-looking criteria (Box 1.1). Banks are required to reclassify loans on a monthly basis rather than on a quarterly, bi-annual or annual basis, as in some other high-income OECD countries (World Bank, 2002) which helps avoid some of the delays in the recognition of credit risks. Also, all loans of a borrower must be classified as problematic if one of the borrower's loans is non-performing, under certain conditions. The IMF (2012a) also points to well-resourced and professional bank supervision, which should support the accuracy of reporting of loan loss. The differences in the composition of exposures classified as "non-problematic" and "problematic" may also suggest prudent classification standards. For example, most exposures to land and all exposures to housing developments which are unfinished but halted are classified as problematic. As a result, the banks recognised losses of 105 billion on these exposures between January 2008 and June 2011 by creating specific provisions and writing off loans.[3] Nonetheless, many loans of intervened banks were reclassified as doubtful after the intervention, pointing to incentives not to recognise losses among weak banks, as pointed out above.

The mortgage loan portfolio is holding up relatively well but there are significant risks ahead

The portfolio of mortgage loans to domestic households accounts for around 60% of GDP and about 15% of bank balance sheets. Despite high unemployment, non-performing loans have remained low. Several factors explain this: low interest rates keep debt servicing costs low, as they are in almost all cases indexed to euro area interbank rates. As a result debt-servicing costs relative to income are close to historic lows (BdE, 2011c). *Second,* incentives for households to service debt are relatively strong, mainly because household loans are full-recourse. Since capital requirements discouraged loan to value ratios in excess of 80% in the boom phase, moderate loan-to-value ratios have also strengthened incentives of households to service debt. Since banks which originated mortgages did not offload associated credit risks through securitisation, incentives for frivolous mortgage lending were contained. For example, banks frequently required multiple personal guarantees to back up loans, notably among family members. These multiple guarantees may also explain why non-performing loans respond relatively little to changes in unemployment in Spain, as empirical research has shown (see IMF, 2012c, and references therein). However, the rise in the share of households in which no adult works has increased and rising long-term unemployment has reduced the coverage of the unemployed with unemployment benefits (Chapter 2). Recent reform of employment protection legislation may also increase the risk that senior household members' debt servicing capacity deteriorates. Moreover, the sharp deterioration of the macroeconomic outlook is also likely to deteriorate asset quality across all loans, including loans to businesses outside the real estate development and construction sector. A further risk are rising interest rates on outstanding mortgage loans, owing to their indexation to short-term interbank rates. This risk will materialise when monetary policy rates go up or risk perceptions in interbank lending rise, with an average lag of 6 months, which is built-in, on average, in interest rate indexation clauses. However, if interest rates were to increase owing to economic recovery in the euro area the recovery would have a positive impact on the Spanish economy, supporting household incomes and mitigating the negative impact of the rise in interest rates.

Market perceptions have deteriorated markedly, drying up wholesale funding

Credit-default swap rates for major Spanish banks have increased sharply since the onset of the euro area debt crisis (Figure 1.8). Banks have satisfied a large share of wholesale funding needs with ECB facilities (Box 1.2). Although market assessments vary across banks, the sharp deterioration has affected all, as funding conditions are constrained by the sovereign's rating. Indeed, the deterioration of market assessments of Spanish banks has occurred in lockstep with the increase in the spreads on sovereign debt. This is reflected in the credit rating of banks, all of which were downgraded sharply in the course of 2012, in line with government ratings. The situation improved somewhat following the ECB's announcement, in September 2012, of the new unlimited bond-buying programme (OMT) in the context of an EFSF or ESM programme.

Figure 1.8. **Recent financial market developments**

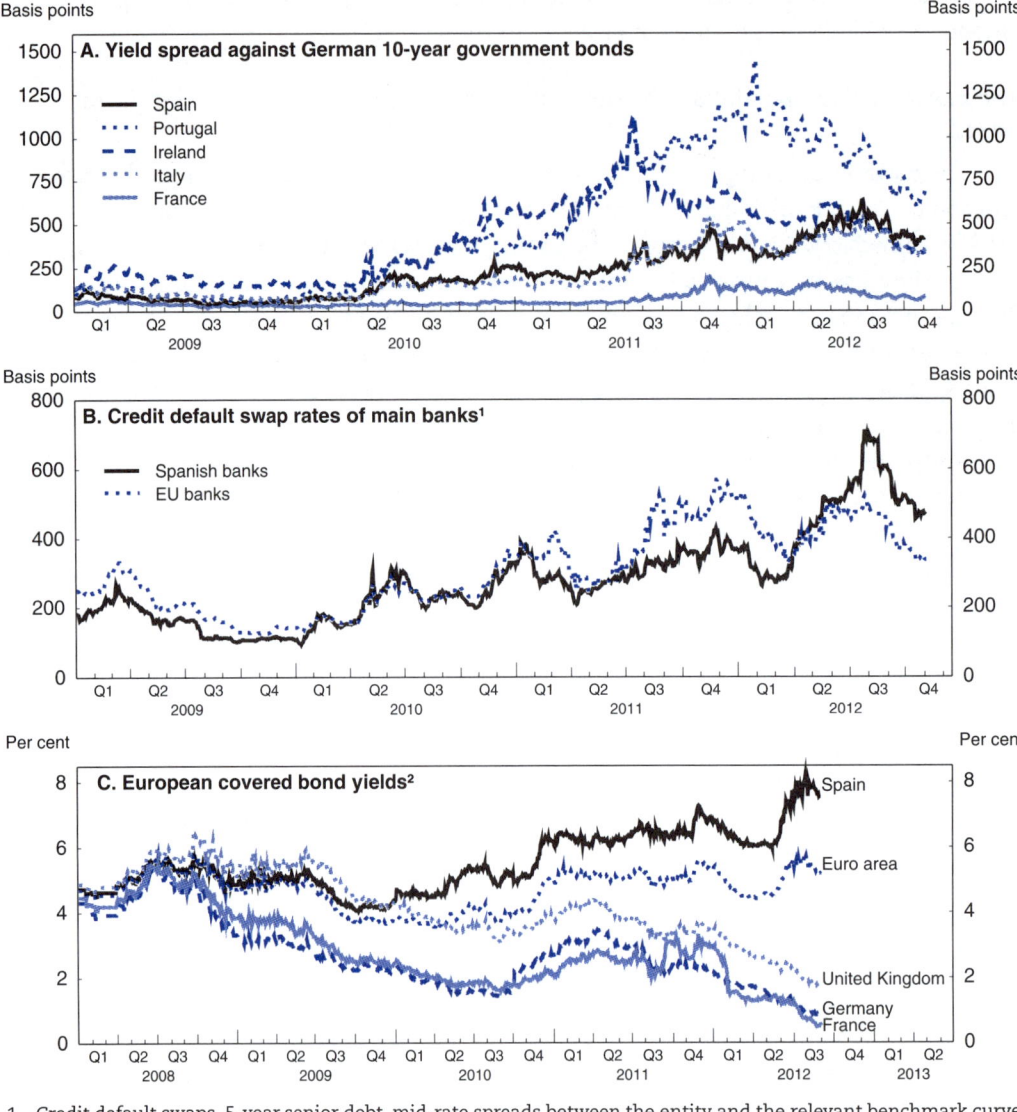

1. Credit default swaps, 5-year senior debt, mid-rate spreads between the entity and the relevant benchmark curve. Spain is an unweighted average of the four main banks. The EU average is calculated by Datastream and includes around 60 banks.
2. Last observation: 30 August 2012.
Source: Datastream Database (2012), November and Bloomberg.

StatLink ᵃᵐˢ₽ *http://dx.doi.org/10.1787/888932740461*

Two factors contribute to the close link between the risk spread on government debt and financial market assessments of the banks. *First*, banks in liquidity and solvency problems have in many cases been bailed out by the national governments in the euro area. Hence, financial markets have transferred increases in government funding costs to bank funding costs and ratings. *Second*, bank holdings of government debt may reinforce this link. Bank holdings of Spanish government debt have risen. Lending to the central government reached 101 billion euros at end-2011, equivalent to 8% of banking system assets and about 40% of central government outstanding debt (IMF, 2012a). However, recent empirical evidence indicates that, within the euro area, the impact of banks' market valuation depended markedly on where the bank's headquarters are located but not on its

Box 1.2. **Liquidity facilities for euro area banks offered by the European Central Bank**

The European Central Bank offered unlimited three-year loans in December 2011 and February 2012. It also reduced the collateral standards for certain asset-backed securities and made room for national central banks within the European Monetary System to widen the collateral further. The credit risk on lending backed up by collateral defined by national central banks is however not born by the ECB but by national governments. The *Banco de España* decided to accept non-collateralised loans of Spanish banks to businesses or public sector entities as collateral, provided the loans are performing and the risk of default is limited to up to 1% according to the *Banco de España's* own valuation.

Spanish banks have borrowed 200 billion euros since 3-year lending facilities were introduced in December 2011, increasing their share of the ECB's net lending (Figure 1.9), absorbing most of the ECB's net lending (gross lending minus deposits). This also reflects the fact that in some countries the banking sector's net borrowing was negative. Most of the borrowers made use of the 3 year facilities. The extension of collateral by the *Banco de España* only accounts for 0.3% of bank borrowing from the ECB. According to estimates of the *Banco de España*, the funds borrowed from the ECB would be sufficient to repay all of bank debt falling due in 2012 and most debt falling due in 2013.

Figure 1.9. **Bank borrowing from ECB**

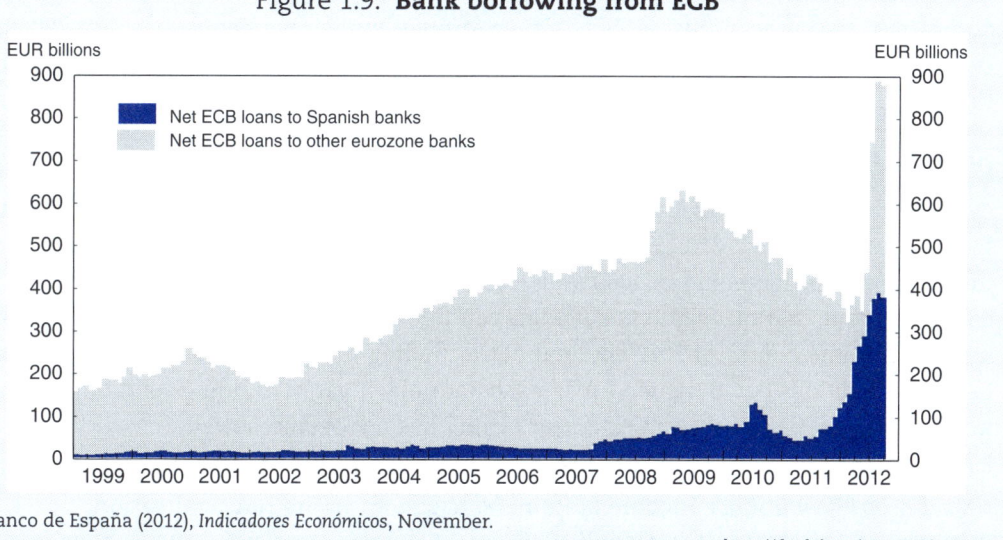

Source: Banco de España (2012), *Indicadores Económicos*, November.

StatLink ⟐⟐⟐ *http://dx.doi.org/10.1787/888932740480*

holdings of Spanish government debt, for example (controlling for some financial indicators of the banks; see Angeloni and Wolff, 2012). This evidence suggests that the government's role as a backstop for the banks is the determining factor, with the market value of banks being depressed in those countries where government's solvency is challenged by the markets. Conversely, perceptions of solvency risks among banks, notably on account of potential losses on their exposures to real estate development, have raised market perceptions of risks to government solvency because of the government resources needed to bail banks out.

The decision of euro area governments to allow for the direct recapitalisation of euro area banks with euro area funds from the European Financial Stability Facility (EFSF) and the European Stability Mechanism (ESM) has the potential to reduce the mutual financial dependency between governments and their banking sectors (see paragraph 1.36 below for details), although it is not yet decided when such recapitalisation will be available. The loan to the Spanish government of up to 100 billion euros, made available by euro area governments to recapitalise Spanish banks, raises Spanish government debt, although the government expects the increase to be limited to about 4% of GDP, in line with the stress tests performed in September 2012 (see below). The government also expects that the loan will be converted into direct recapitalisation with European funds, without impact on government debt, once the common euro area bank supervision framework has been put in place.

Deposits held by residents in the private non-financial sector have been on a modestly declining trend between mid-2011 and July 2012. Part of the deposit outflows appear to be accounted for by clients' purchases of commercial paper from their banks which offered higher interest and, to a lesser extent, by household purchases of government bonds. Banks offered commercial paper to their clients in reaction to the increase in contributions banks had to pay to the compulsory deposit insurance fund for high-yield deposits. The government introduced this increase in 2011 in order to prevent banks from competing for deposits by raising interest rates, although this decision has recently been reversed. Commercial paper is not subject to contributions. Declining gross financial wealth of households and non-financial businesses also contributed to lower deposits. Deposits domestic non-financial businesses held at foreign banks rose somewhat (BdE, 2012c). Deposits held by foreign economic agents at Spanish banks diminished more markedly. However, non-financial business deposits are typically volatile.

Diminished profitability will keep lending conditions tight

According to the ECB's loan officers' survey, lending conditions have tightened further throughout the period 2010-12, especially for long-term lending (including mortgages), on top of the sharp tightening in 2008 and 2009. Since the last quarter of 2011 the share of banks reporting that they tightened lending conditions because of poor funding conditions has risen. In the course of 2012 abundant ECB funding has prevented further tightening. Lending conditions could tighten further substantially if banks' funding conditions do not improve, especially since the ECB's 3 year facility has not been renewed.

The banks reported losses on aggregate in 2011 following the substantial downward revision of BFA-Bankia's income statement triggered by its nationalisation (Box 1.3), reflecting deteriorating asset quality. In the near term provisioning will continue to generate losses. In addition, the average interest margin has declined from 1.4 to about 1% between 2009 and 2011. Margins have stabilised more recently, reflecting the large volume of cheap ECB funding as well as rising interest rates on new lending. However, withdrawal of some of the large amount of liquidity supplied by the ECB would raise the need for market-based funding and could therefore raise funding costs of the banks, putting more pressure on margins. Banks have responded by reducing capacity, with employment and the number of branches falling by about 10% between 2009 and 2011. While the branch network is unusually dense in Spain, the share of banking services in economy-wide employment is lower than in the other large European economies.

Box 1.3. **The nationalisation of BFA-Bankia**

BFA-Bankia is one of two big savings banks groups which belong to the four biggest banks in Spain, with consolidated assets of about 320 billion euros (9% of aggregate consolidated banks' assets or about 30% of GDP). It was created by merging 7 savings banks, including several institutions which were heavily exposed to the residential construction boom, notably the biggest involved in the merger, *Caja Madrid*. Bankia, an incorporated subsidiary of BFA, was floated on the stock exchange in 2011, as part of a business plan presented to the authorities to meet tighter capital requirements. To make BFA more attractive to investors, assets most exposed to housing market risks were kept outside Bankia on BFA's balance sheet, while most banking business was transferred to Bankia. The new stockholders took a minority share with BFA retaining control. Following the refusal of the bank's auditor to approve the 2011 accounts, shortfalls in core capital became evident which the bank could not address, resulting in the resignation of the chairperson. As a first step, a convertible bond of 4½ billion euros (0.4% of GDP), which had previously been purchased by the government's Fund for the Orderly Restructuring of Banks (*Fondo de Reestructuración Ordenada Bancaria*, FROB) to support restructuring in the savings banks sector, was converted into common equity. The government signaled it would provide any amount the capital needed for a viable business plan. The new management then revised the 2011 accounts (beyond the requirements of the auditor) and requested an additional capital injection of 19 billion euros. According to a statement issued by BFA this amount covers additional provisions on its exposures to real estate risks (13 billion, of which 9 billion to absorb the new provisioning requirements introduced in 2012 and 4 billion in excess of the new requirements), risks on other loan portfolios resulting from the adverse macroeconomic prospects (5½ billion euros) and a write-down of deferred tax assets and stakes in firms to market prices (6½ billion euros). All these losses were applied to 2011 results. They lead the group to present a loss of 3½ billion euros for 2011 and negative equity of the consolidated group balance sheet of 4½ billion euros, putting the group *a posteriori* in a situation of technical insolvency. The equity holdings of the seven constituent savings banks of BFA are hence likely to be wiped out, whereas a diluted minority private stake of Bankia will remain. Following the group's announcement of further losses in the first half of 2012 the FROB provided an immediate capital injection of 4.5 billion euros.

The government has taken steps to strengthen the resilience of the banking sector

Government financial support has been limited until recently

Since 2009, the government provided capital injections to support merger processes among savings banks and to help banks reach tightening capital and provisioning requirements (see further below). Prior to the partial nationalisation of the savings banks group BFA-Bankia in May 2012, capital injections amounted to 13 billion euros (1.2% of GDP) all to savings banks or their subsidiaries. Further financial support to failing banks has been given by the deposit insurance fund in the context of the resolution of failed banks. These require further capital injections before they are resolved. However, the deposit insurance fund, while legally mandated and regulated, is owned and managed by the banks.

The government has also supplied explicit guarantees to bank issuance of senior bonds of maturity of up to 5 years. This liquidity support has been open to all banks, although banks pay a commission to the government of up to 105 basis points, depending on their credit rating. Outstanding guarantees amounted to 97 billion euros in March 2012. For the full year 2012, banks can issue 100 billion euros of senior debt with government guarantees, of which 4.2 billion had been issued by February. The guarantee programme has however 2 important disadvantages. *First*, it supports mainly weak entities, as the gap between the funding costs of strong banks and the government is relatively small. This support may therefore reinforce the undesirable effect the presence of weak banks has on the economy (see above). *Second*, it raises potential losses of the holders of unguaranteed bank debt in case of bank resolution, especially in the context of the adoption of a bail-in policy in resolution, so may crowd out private funding of banks. The bank debt guarantee programme should be phased out as soon as possible once the most solvent banks have regained access to wholesale funding markets.

The government has accelerated loss recognition

Financial market reforms introduced in February and May 2012 raised the buffers banks have to create to be able to absorb losses on their exposures to domestic real estate. Public capital injections are offered to banks deemed viable but unable to meet the new requirements. Banks are also given some incentives to merge (Box 1.4). The reforms include further steps to improve transparency on the financial situation of banks and changes in savings bank governance, discussed further below.

Banks were required to build up provisions and specific capital buffers of about 83 billion euros (8% of GDP) to cover potential losses on loans to construction and real estate development exposures. Most of these buffers will add to the provisions created for this purpose by the end of 2011, although banks may convert the existing stock of "dynamic provisions" (1% of GDP at end-2011) to specific provisions in order to satisfy the new requirements. Overall they are expected to increase to 137 billion (14% of GDP) by December 2012, covering almost one half of the total exposure, leaving exposures worth about 15% of GDP uncovered (Table 1.1). Most of the 7 largest banks have met the requirements quickly, drawing on current earnings, the conversion of convertible obligations and excess reserves, although in the case of BFA-Bankia these have been met with a large government capital injection.

Among the large components of the problematic exposures, land is most extensively covered, as land markets have collapsed the most. Exposures to problematic finished housing are less well-covered, with banks being able to absorb 54% of price falls on average without incurring losses. The coverage of exposures to finished housing which have not, so far, been classified as problematic is also the lowest, at 14%, and this exposure is large, amounting to 60 billion euros. Following its partial nationalisation, BFA considered necessary to create provisions on real estate exposures somewhat in excess of the new requirements. Moreover, the case of BFA-Bankia illustrates that there is a need to address loan losses that result from the deterioration of the economic outlook since 2011, which will raise loan losses in other loan segments.

Restructuring of savings banks has had mixed results

Reforms in 2009 and 2010 had a substantial impact on savings bank governance and the structure of the sector (see OECD, 2010). Mergers and the resolution of a few entities have reduced the number of savings banks from 45 to 9. Most of the mergers were supported by government capital injections. Virtually all savings banks have made use of the option to transfer their business to an incorporated subsidiary bank. Several

Box 1.4. **Measures to strengthen buffers against real estate exposures in the February and May 2012 financial reforms**

Provisioning and capital buffers

25 billion euros of provisions and 15 billion euros of specific capital surcharges are introduced for exposures classified as "problematic", raising their coverage to around 60% on average.

- **Exposures to land:** Coverage with specific provisions is raised from 31% on average at end-2011 to at least 60%. A capital surcharge of 20% is introduced.

- **Exposures to unfinished housing:** Provisions are raised from 27% on average to at least 50% in most cases (loans backed up by such projects which are performing but nonetheless classified as problematic must be provisioned by only 24%). The capital surcharge amounts to 15% of the book value.

- **Exposures to finished housing:** Loans backed up by such housing must be provisioned by 25 to 30% in all cases, depending on the extent of impairment. Finished real estate foreclosed from construction or real estate businesses must be provisioned according to a progressive schedule depending on the length of time it has been held, rising from 25% in the first year to 50% in the fourth year (previously, these provisions ranged from 10% in the first year to 30% in the third year).

- **Housing foreclosed from households** (main residences) must be provisened by 10% every year it is held by the bank, up to 40% (up to 30% previously).

As before the reform, foreclosed real estate must be valued by the lower of the transaction price and the appraisal price as assessed by independent appraisal companies (*tasadores*) at the time of the foreclosure.

As a result of these buffers banks will be able to absorb a cumulated decline in prices on land of around 90%, on average, before such price declines affect banks' general capital buffers according to estimates from the *Banco de España*. For finished housing, they can absorb price declines of 54%.

Banks must generally meet these requirements by end-2012. The rules mostly apply to positions outstanding at the end of 2011 so as to avoid discouraging new lending.

Further provisioning requirements are introduced for loans not classified as problematic. These amount to 25 billion and raise coverage to 30% on average. Exposures to land must be covered by 52%, exposures to uncompleted housing projects by 29% and exposures to completed housing by 14%. Plans to meet these requirements in full, including measures to cover any resulting capital shortfalls, must be implemented by October 2012.

Incentives for mergers

Incentives are provided for banks to meet the requirements through mergers. Banks announcing mergers by June 2012 are eligible to an extension of the deadline to meet the new rules to June 2013. Mergers must be completed by January 2013. Merged banks can book provisions directly against equity of the merged institution. To qualify, mergers must be approved by the government and must raise the bigger bank's balance sheet by at least 20%.

Government support

Banks who fail to meet capital requirements following the application of the provisions can receive support from the dedicated government fund, the FROB, provided the *Banco de España* approves their business plan (see OECD, 2010 for a detailed description of responsibilities of the FROB). Recipients must improve corporate governance and present plans to divest foreclosed real estate. Stricter divestment requirements have been set in the Memorandum of Understanding which lists the conditions applying to the disbursement. The FROB will be able to purchase ordinary shares from banks and hold them for a maximum of three years. It can also purchase contingent convertible bonds from merging banks. These must be bought back by the banks or converted into ordinary equity within 5 years and will carry an interest rate of 10%.

Table 1.1. **Exposures to construction and real estate development (including housing foreclosed from households)**

Per cent of GDP

	Exposure	Covered exposure
Normal	12	5
Problematic	17	9
Total	**29**	**14**

Source: Ministry of Economy and Banco de España.

subsidiaries have issued shares, diluting the savings bank holding's ownership of the banking business. If the savings bank loses control or its share in the subsidiary drops below 25% it has to transform itself into holding foundations with no banking licence.

The consolidation process resulted in a reduction of employment and bank offices by 17% since 2008. However, some mergers resulted in financially weak banks. Several of them had to be nationalised (such as BFA-Bankia) or intervened and sold off subsequently (see the discussion of bank resolution below). In the meantime, they are likely to have weakened confidence in the financial system as a whole, in part due to the financial links among banks. Moreover, there is evidence that economies of scale and scope are small in banking beyond a relatively small size, suggesting mergers do not improve efficiency (Bouis and Cournède, 2012 and references therein). Mergers may also create more banks which are too-big-to fail, potentially raising financial risks for the government.

The influence of regional and local policy makers on savings banks has declined as a result of the creation of banking subsidiaries, the entry of private investors in their corporate subsidiaries and nationalisation. This influence may decline further in the future as the central government divests its capital injections, which include non-voting participations. However, with the exception of nationalised banks, most savings banks have so far retained majority control of their subsidiaries. The voting shares of regional and local governments in the savings banks' general assemblies remain large. They are limited to 40% but local and regional governments may effectively control larger voting rights, for example, via the representation of the savings banks' founders. Their commercial bank subsidiaries may also have close managerial ties with savings bank holding groups. The influence of regional and local policy makers on savings banks should be further reduced. Full loss recognition and comprehensive recapitalisation of these banks, a key priority in itself, will reduce such influence in many cases. As long as savings banks exercise control over banking activities, management of the commercial banks should be kept at arms' length from their savings bank holdings, as recommended in the IMF's FSAP, for example, by requiring savings bank management to abstain from managing banking subsidiaries and ensuring the independence of non-executive board members. Moreover the independence of management of the savings banks from local political influence should be strengthened, for example by introducing fit-and-proper tests for all savings bank senior management, as recommended in the IMF's FSAP (IMF, 2012d).

Capital requirements have anticipated Basel III rules

As part of the conditionality attached to the recapitalisation of Spanish banks with euro area funds, the EBA's requirement of a 9% common equity capital ratio will be extended to all banks from January 2013. This will not imply a substantial tightening of existing rules. In the previous regime, since 2011, all banks had been required to hold at least 8% of "principal capital" relative to risk-weighted assets. The requirement rises to 10% for those banks which cover 20% or more of their funding needs on wholesale markets and have not sold at least 10% of their capital to outside investors. The definition of principal capital is close to the definition of common equity capital in *Basel III* in its transitional mode, as applicable from 2013 onwards.[4] The requirements are above the minimum *Basel III* requirement of 4.5% and the *Basel III* requirement including the capital conservation buffer of 7%. The average "principal capital" adequacy ratio to risk-weighted assets Spanish banks held end-2011 reached about 10%. Given the minimum "principal capital" requirements in place since 2011, few banks have significantly worse capital ratios than the average (BdE, 2012b).

Euro area governments will provide funds to recapitalise banks on the basis of comprehensive stress tests

In June 2012, the government requested financial assistance for the recapitalisation of Spanish banks from euro area governments. The euro area governments agreed to provide a loan facility to the government of up to 100 billion euros (9½ per cent of GDP). The loan will initially be funded by the EFSF and will subsequently be taken over by the ESM once it is operational. On the basis of the current agreement, the loan contributes to public debt but does not have seniority over other government creditors in case of default. Moreover, the euro area governments agreed that euro area banks can be recapitalised by the ESM directly, rather than via a loan to the government, once a common supervisory mechanism for the euro area banks is in place. The Spanish government expects the loan to be replaced by the direct recapitalisation of the banks by the ESM once a common supervisory framework of euro area banks is agreed. The disbursement of the loan is subject to conditions which focus on financial sector policies, set out in a Memorandum of Understanding (MoU, Box 1.5).

Stress testing to identify capital needs for the banking sector at an aggregate level ("top-down") was conducted in the IMF's FSAP and by two consultancy firms contracted by the government, followed up by an independent detailed stress-test on the whole portfolio of individual banks ("bottom-up"), which was conducted between June and September 2012 (Box 1.6). The "bottom-up"stress testing exercise has been comprehensive and takes into account detailed information of balance sheets and loan portfolios of individual banks. It has been conducted under the supervision of European Union institutions (the European Commission, the ECB and the European Banking Authority) and the International Monetary Fund, and provides a solid assessment of the capital needs. Overall, the stress tests point to moderate capital needs of up to 6% of GDP for the most adverse scenario contemplated in the exercise. As the recent evolution in Spain shows, feedback mechanisms between bank asset quality and economic activity can result in macroeconomic outcomes and asset impairment that are considerably worse than anticipated earlier on. Such feedback mechanisms have been particularly important in the context of the euro area crisis. The Spanish authorities should stand ready to react in the future if the economic situation deteriorates significantly beyond the prudent stress test assumptions.

The banks where capital needs have been identified under the adverse scenario of the "bottom-up" stress testing exercise were required to submit recapitalisation plans to the Spanish authorities in mid-October. These plans set out how the requirements identified in the "bottom-up" assessments will be met. Banks requiring public funds will be required to develop a restructuring plan, to be approved by the Spanish authorities and the

Box 1.5. **Conditions on financial sector policies in the Memorandum of Understanding**

A memorandum of understanding sets out the conditions the Spanish authorities and the banks must meet to receive the EFSF and ESM funds for their recapitalisation. The European Commission (EC), the European Central Bank and the International Monetary Fund (IMF) will monitor progress with meeting these requirements and the provision of the necessary data.

Recapitalisation of viable banks, resolution of non-viable banks

Following identification of capital needs in the "bottom-up" stress testing (see above) the authorities will present restructuring plans for viable banks requiring recapitalisation with public funds and resolution plans for non-viable banks. The resolution plans should minimise costs to taxpayers and will provide for the transfer of balance sheet positions to solid banks through competitive processes. Restructuring and resolution plans will have to be presented to the European Commission, the European Central Bank and the International Monetary Fund for approval by December (by November for banks which were already nationalised before the loan programme). Banks which can meet their capital needs from private sources have until June 2013 to do so.

Burden sharing

The Spanish authorities are required to minimise costs to tax payers from resolution and restructuring by allocating losses to equity, hybrid capital and subordinate debt holders in all banks requiring public capital injections to the full extent possible while protecting deposits. Legislation must be introduced to enable mandatory bail-in of hybrid capital and subordinated debt instruments (*i.e.* require owners of such instruments to absorb losses) and improve resolution mechanisms. The *Banco de España* is required to monitor that banks do not repurchase such instruments at market price plus 10%.

Segregation of impaired assets

All banks receiving public capital injections are required to move problematic assets, especially those related to real estate development, into a centralised asset management company. The assets will be priced at their "real (long term) economic value", on the basis of the independent valuations carried out by the audit companies. The asset management company may hold the assets over extended periods to avoid losses. The exposure of banks to the risks will be limited to a small equity share in the asset management company. They will receive long-term bonds issued by the FROB, which are in turned guaranteed and financed by the Spanish government. The financial risks of the assets transferred will therefore largely remain with the government.

Improvements in the regulatory framework

All Spanish banks will be required to hold 9% common equity relative to risk-weighted assets. The authorities are required to review permanent provisioning rules, including a recalibration of the statistical provisioning regime. Further improvements in the governance of savings banks groups are required, to further reduce the influence of savings banks on their corporate subsidiaries and improve their management. Non-listed savings bank groups will have to become listed. Consumer protection must be strengthened to avoid mis-selling of risky bank-issued securities to retail investors.

Improvements in the supervisory framework

The independence of the supervisor, *the Banco de España*, must be improved, including by strengthening its powers to issue sanctions and regulations. The supervisor is also required to identity improvements in internal procedures so as to ensure that findings of inspectors translate into prompt corrective action.

Box 1.6. **Stress testing exercises**

"Top-down" stress tests in the IMF FSAP 2012

The tests cover 95% of the domestic banking sector, using end-2011 supervisory information. The adverse scenario includes a cumulative decline of real GDP 5.7 percentage points in 2012 and 2013 (the OECD Secretariat projects real GDP to fall by about 3%) and a decline of house prices of 23% over the same period. The scenarios include valuation haircuts on sovereign debt held in trading portfolios only, as sovereign bonds can be used to obtain liquidity from the central bank, which reduces pressure to sell. The capital needs to comply with a 7% core Tier 1 ratio (the *Basel III* requirement) in this scenario amount to 20-37 billion euros (2-3½ per cent of GDP). Most of the capital needs concern savings bank groups which had previously been intervened or had received government help. The IMF team concluded that "while the core of the system appears resilient, there are vulnerabilities that need to be addressed." The IMF's stress tests did not take into account the merger of several small-to-medium-sized banks from the savings bank sector with large solvent banks, which may have reduced recapitalisation needs.

"Top-down" stress tests of 2 private consultancy firms on the request of the Spanish authorities (June 2012)

2 private consultancy firms conducted tests separately, but using the same assumptions. The adverse scenario includes a cumulative decline in real GDP of 6.5% from 2012 to 2014 (the OECD projects a decline of 2.2%) and a decline in house prices of 25.5%. The tests covered 90% of the domestic banking sector using data as of end-2011. They incorporated more detailed supervisory information than the IMF FSAP and took into account mergers in the first months of 2012.

According to one consultancy firm, the capital needs to comply with a 6% core Tier 1 ratio in this scenario amount to 51-62 billion euros (5-6% of GDP) and to 52 billion euros according to the other consultancy firm. According to the *Banco de España* the differences in the result with respect to the IMF FSAP are explained by the differences of assumptions, notably the longer time horizon and more adverse scenario in the case of the consultancy firms.

"Bottom-up" stress tests on the request of the Spanish authorities

An independent detailed stress-test of the balance sheets of individual banks was conducted between June and September 2012 by a private consultancy firm and benefited from the work of four auditing firms and six independent appraisal companies. It was supervised by the Spanish authorities, European Union institutions (The European Commission, the ECB and the European Banking Authority) and the International Monetary Fund. The macroeconomic scenarios considered and the target capital ratios are the same as in the "top-down" stress tests of the 2 private consultancy firms (see above). Under the adverse scenario 7 banking groups representing 38% of the banking sector would need 53.8 billion euros (5% of GDP) more capital, once ongoing mergers and some tax effects are taken into account, and 59 billion euros without considering projected mergers.

European Commission. The banks will have to meet their capital needs within 9 months. Banks requiring recapitalisation with public funds are required to transfer impaired assets, notably those related to real estate, to an asset management company.

Steps have been taken to accelerate the restructuring and resolution of banks

Since the outbreak of the international financial crisis in 2008, the *Banco de España* has intervened 5 small and medium-sized banks (Box 1.7) because they did not meet regulatory standards or because they failed to present adequate business plans to overcome risks to their viability. They were subsequently offered for tender. Some have been sold off to other domestic banks, effectively at a negative price, while the process is still pending for 2 banks. All were closely linked to the savings bank sector. The larger institutions were intervened in 2011, relatively late in the economic and financial crisis.

Box 1.7. **Intervention and resolution of banks in the current crisis**

The *Banco de España* and the FROB intervened 5 banks: 3 small banks (*Caja Castilla la Mancha* in 2008; *Cajasur* in 2009; *Unnim*, 2011) and two medium-sized banks (*Caja Mediterráneo, Banco de Valencia*, in 2011). Three further banks were nationalised without being intervened, with the government obtaining control through capital injections. Apart from BFA-Bankia, this applies to *Catalunya Banc* and *NCG Banco*, both medium-sized subsidiaries of savings banks groups. All these banks were savings banks or their subsidiaries.

Four of these banks have been taken over by other domestic banks. In three cases (*Unnim, Cam* with consolidated assets worth 100 billion euros, 3% of the banking system), the transaction effectively involved a negative price. Purchase offers were selected through a tendering process so as to minimise costs and risks to the fund. The banks' deposit insurance fund has born most of the resulting losses which amounted to 7.9 billion euros (0.7% of GDP). It will also cover 80% of losses on a portfolio of problematic loans over a period of 10 years. These guarantees cover assets (net of provisions) with an accounting value of 28 billion euros (2½ per cent of GDP). The government also ensured liquidity provision to failing banks. Two banks (*Catalunya Banc* and *Banco de Valencia*) were offered for tender in April 2012, and the same is planned for *NCG Banco* after its savings bank holding withdrew its right to repurchase the FROB's shares. These 3 banks, for which resolution is pending, have consolidated assets of about 170 billion euros (5% of the banking system). The government has injected about 6½ billion euros of capital and has issues guarantees for assets worth 3½ billion euros in these banks, while the deposit insurance fund has provided a capital injection of 2 billion euros. A further capital injection of 9 billion euros will be necessary to cover the stricter provisioning requirements on real estate exposures introduced in 2012.

In order to fund the absorption of these losses, contributions to the banks' own deposit insurance funds were raised to 0.2 per cent of deposits and legislation was introduced to raise these contributions to 3 per thousand if necessary. The deposit insurance fund's assets declined from a peak of 8.5 billion euros in 2008 to 5.5 billion euros at the end of 2011.

The resulting losses were largely born by the banks' own deposit insurance fund. As in earlier banking crisis the deposit insurance fund, which is legally mandated, has funded the resolution of failed banks, in addition to providing deposit insurance. The asset stock of the deposit insurance fund diminished markedly as a result and the contributions banks pay to the fund, which are assessed on the balance of bank deposits, had to be raised. It is appropriate to fund costs of bank resolution, to the extent they cannot be born by shareholders or creditors, with contributions paid by the banks. However, these contributions should be separated from the contributions to deposit insurance and should be assessed on the total of bank balance sheets as it is a more appropriate measure of the potential cost the failure of a bank may generate.

Improving resolution mechanisms is an important element of the international agenda of financial market reform to reduce the need for tax revenues to bail out failing banks (FSB, 2011). The European Commission prepared a proposal for a directive to improve resolution throughout the European Union in 2012, which will take substantial time to be implemented. However, early introduction of reform steps accelerates bank restructuring and reduces the impact of losses in bank balance sheets on government debt. For this reason, it is appropriate that the MoU required the Spanish authorities to present legislation to facilitate bank resolution in August 2012. Indeed, the resolution authorities' powers fell short of the *Key Attributes of Effective Bank Resolution* issued by the Financial Stability Board in a number of areas. These areas included powers to override shareholder rights of failing banks (such as in the approval of transactions), to transfer assets as well as to carry out "bail-ins" of all equity and of unsecured debt (*i.e.* force the owners of equity and debt to absorb losses) without triggering formal bankruptcy. A decree-law to facilitate bank resolution and to reinforce intervention powers in a banking crisis was hence approved by the government on 31 August 2012 and entered into force immediately (Box 1.8). The legislation should be used to override shareholder rights of banks in resolution, for example, to avoid that incumbent shareholders hold up decisions of the resolution authorities on the transfer of assets of banks and to impose losses on creditors. As a complementary measure, it would be desirable to introduce preferential treatment of deposits in the hierarchy of creditors especially if senior debt is bailed-in, so as to make clear that deposits are not included in such bail-ins. Co-ordinated introduction of depositor preference in the euro area would be preferable.

Bank resolution has so far involved wiping out holders of common equity. Debt, including subordinate debt, has generally been fully bailed out, including hybrid instruments with subordination clauses which count as Tier I capital, such as preferential shares. The authorities have avoided forcing creditors to take losses in order to prevent contagion risk and because of consumer protection concerns, as many banks have sold preferential shares and subordinate debt to their retail customers, in some cases perhaps without providing transparent information about the risks. However, about half of subordinate debt issued by Spanish banks has been subscribed by institutional investors, where consumer protection concerns do not apply. To reduce the potential costs of resolution for the government or the banking system (through the deposit insurance fund) the authorities should bail in selected holders of bank debt. This policy should also be applied to absorb losses of banks which are recapitalised rather than resolved orderly, as foreseen in the MoU and in the resolution legislation introduced in August 2012. The repurchase or write-down of subordinate debt or hybrid capital on the basis of market prices only, as foreseen in the new resolution legislation, may not be fully satisfactory, as market conditions may be difficult to observe and market prices depend on the perceived bail-in policy. Conversion into equity may be preferable. In any case it should be ensured that the full nominal value of these debt instruments is available for loss absorption.

If bail-ins are limited to subordinated debt and lower-ranking instruments contagion risks are likely to be limited. Such bailing-in might, at worst, prevent the issuance of subordinate debt. The issuance of new subordinate debt has become less important for banks with the adoption of the *Basel III* framework, which has reinforced the role of

> ### Box 1.8. **Legislation to restructure and resolve banks introduced in August 2012**
>
> A decree-law to facilitate bank resolution and to reinforce intervention powers in a banking crisis was approved by the government on 31 August 2012 and entered into force immediately. It defines the powers of the *Banco de España* and the *Fondo de Reestructuración Ordenada Bancaria* (FROB) to: i) take preventive action when risks arise that banks may not meet regulatory requirements; ii) restructure banks which need public support to ensure their viabililty; and iii) resolve banks deemed non-viable. Measures to restructure banks in need of public support include the transfer of impaired assets to an asset management company. In the case of non-viable banks, the FROB takes over the management and develops a resolution plan. The authorities can selectively transfer assets and liabilities of such a bank to a temporary bridge bank and to an asset management company without requiring shareholder consent. The law also empowers the authorities to impose losses on creditors of banks which are restructured or resolved. However, such loss-absorption ("bail-in") is limited to hybrid capital instruments and subordinated debt, excluding senior debt. Bail-ins can be carried out by converting such debt instruments into equity as well as by repurchasing them or by writing down their nominal value on the basis of market prices. The FROB can also modify other rights of owners of such debt, such as by postponing the contractual maturity.
>
> The legislation modifies the governance of the FROB, doing away with the role the deposit insurance played in it previously (OECD, 2010). The board of the FROB will consist of representatives of the government, who will hold the majority, and the *Banco de España*. It will be funded by the government and by its own debt issuance, subject to limits defined in the law.
>
> The new legislation also includes provisions concerning the set-up of an asset management company for the transfer of impaired assets, capital requirements, consumer protection, powers to sanction banks infringing regulation, executive pay of managers of banks receiving public aid as well as extended regulatory powers to strengthen the independence of the *Banco de España* as a bank regulator and supervisor.

highest-quality common equity and reduced the role of tier II capital (to which subordinated debt generally belongs) in meeting capital requirements. Moreover, by reducing the cost of bank resolution to the public purse, such a step could also strengthen the capacity of the government to credibly support key systemic banking sector functions, such as bank deposits. Outstanding subordinate debt buffers are substantial, amounting to 86 billion euros at end-2011. Such bail-ins should be used for the resolution of failed banks and for the absorption of losses in insolvent banks which are rescued by the government and maintained as going concerns. In the context of comprehensive bank restructuring, in which all non-viable banks are closed and viable banks comprehensively recapitalised, potential fiscal costs could be reduced further by imposing losses on senior debt, in addition to subordinated debt, for banks in orderly resolution. For this case, in particular, the bail-in framework needs to be carefully designed (IMF, 2012e). Ideally it should be activated when a capital infusion is expected, with official liquidity support as a backstop until the bank is stabilised.

In all cases of bail-in, where consumer protection concerns exist, a smaller haircut should be imposed on affected households with small investments. The *core principles* of the FSA provide room for treating holders of the same type of debt differently. To preserve legal certainty, a two-step procedure could be followed. In a first stage bail-in would proceed without discrimination. In a second stage, legal recourse on consumer protection grounds could be allowed for small bondholders. Alternatively, the government could bail out small bondholders immediately. The government should then take judicial actions against the banks that violated consumers' rights. To prevent recurrence of such concerns in the future, it is important to investigate responsibilities of bank management in breaking consumer protection rules and review the effectiveness of consumer protection rules to avoid future occurrence. Legislation introduced in August 2012 requires 50% of new issues must be sold to wholesale investors. It also introduces minimum thresholds for retail investments in such instruments.

Banks have recently reduced hybrid capital and subordinated debt buffers by buying back such instruments or transforming them into deposits, including in cases where such instruments are held by institutional investors, perhaps in order to protect their relationships with clients or raise reported profits. This may in some cases have reduced the availability of these instruments for loss absorption, especially when resolution or public recapitalisation is likely in the near future. The authorities should be proactive in preventing any payouts or repurchases of capital when the capacity of loss-absorption is compromised. Their conversion in equity is desirable. Banks' operations reducing their hybrid capital and subordinated debt buffers should be closely supervised and stopped if these operations reduce the amount of funds available for absorbing losses. More generally, the supervisor should ban any payouts (including through the buy-back of equity) from banks, including savings banks, in which it would be prudent to strengthen capital positions. The bank supervisor, the *Banco de España*, needs to be endowed with the powers to take such action. The provision in Memorandum of Understanding, which requires the *Banco de España* to stop banks which may need public support from repurchasing subordinate debt instruments at above market price + 10% may not be satisfactory, as market conditions may be difficult to observe and market prices depend on the perceived bail-in policy.

The *Banco de España* has replaced senior management in intervened institutions and the government has limited compensation of management of banks which receive government capital injections from the FROB to at most 1.2 million euros or 2 annual salaries.[5] However, these limits may not be ambitious enough. For example, they do not apply to managers appointed after banks receive government financial assistance, even if the bank is bailed out subsequently. Moreover, the bank supervisor (the *Banco de España*) does not have powers to supervise compensation packages generally. Appropriate compensation payments are of key importance for managerial incentives and high compensation for parting managers is a source of moral hazard. Compensation packages should be supervised by the bank supervisor. It should have powers to claw back compensation payments of managers of entities which are resolved or bailed out by government, as recommended by the Financial Stability Board (FSB, 2011).

Separation of legacy assets from vulnerable banks is appropriate

The MoU requires the separation of legacy assets from all banks in need of public support in a dedicated asset management company. Legislation introduced in August 2012 provides the legal basis for setting up an asset management company and steps have been taken to set it up and transfer assets to it. Separating the management of legacy assets from banking business is useful to improve investor confidence in the banks and focus bank management on the lending and deposit-taking business. The legislation requires that private capital contributes to the funding of the asset management company. In particular, more than 50% of the company's assets must be owned by private agents. Its debt will therefore not be considered as government debt. However, most funding needs will be covered with the issuance of bonds guaranteed by the Spanish government, which exposes the government to financial risks. It is therefore important that the prices at which legacy assets are transferred are conservatively priced. The MoU foresees that legacy assets be priced at "long-term economic value" which risks pricing them above what current market conditions warrant. A relatively high transfer price also risks reducing the extent to which bank creditors take losses, even though the *Key Attributes of Effective Resolution Regimes* stipulate that owners of bailed-in bank debt need not recover more funds than they would in case of liquidation, in which case current market prices would apply. One option to reduce the need for the government to bear associated risks would be to use bank debt that has been selected for loss absorption to help fund the transfer of assets from a bank with solvency problems to the asset management company which is dedicated to taking over its impaired real-estate related assets, although this may require some decentralisation of the asset management structure to the individual bank level. Both a centralised structure and decentralised companies set-up at the level of each bank are conceivable (IMF, 2002).

Effective bankruptcy regimes can accelerate loss recognition and strengthen structural change

Effective bankruptcy procedures can support deleveraging processes (IMF, 2002). They can accelerate the identification of businesses and households who are not in a position to repay debt and improve the reallocation of physical capital and loanable funds, preventing them from being locked in non-viable businesses. They can also put more pressure on weak banks to recognise losses in the loan portfolio, accelerating bank restructuring. Efficient bankruptcy procedures also help the creditors recover loans from insolvent firms, in part by facilitating an appropriate decision to either liquidate a firm, or help it remain active by restructuring its debt burden. The experience of Chile has shown that reform of bankruptcy legislation can play a significant role in the deleveraging process (Bouis and Cournède, 2012). Bankruptcy procedures can also help households and entrepreneurs make a "fresh start", following insolvency, by providing incentives to resume economic activity in the formal economy and can help avoid unnecessary hardship among households. It can also encourage entrepreneurship, including by preserving human capital of failed entrepreneurs. Business conduct of non-financial firms and banks is substantially affected by bankruptcy codes. For example empirical evidence (Davidenko and Franks, 2008) indicates that bankruptcy regimes which make the recovery of loans from insolvent firms more difficult require more collateral from borrowers than elsewhere. There is substantial evidence that opportunities for discharge can improve entrepreneurship (Mora-Sanguinetti and Fuentes, 2012, and references therein).

In international comparison, recourse to bankruptcy among non-financial firms is unusually low in Spain (Table 1.2). There are some indications that bankruptcy procedures are inefficient, which may reduce their use by creditors or debtors, even though, for insolvent debtors, under certain conditions, starting such procedures is a legal obligation. Creditor protection is rated lower than in a majority of OECD countries according to an indicator developed by Porter *et al*. The recovery of debt of firms in bankruptcy appears to be relatively low even though few firms undergoing bankruptcy procedures appear to escape liquidation (see Mora and Fuentes, 2012, for some evidence).

Table 1.2. **Business bankruptcies per 10 000 firms**

2006

	Bankrupty rate		Bankruptcy rate
Poland	1.79	Netherlands	79.60
Spain	**2.56**	Japan	86.59
Czech Republic	5.43	Norway	95.51
Greece	6.81	Germany	96.31
South Korea	7.78	Finland	96.64
Portugal	15.01	Belgium	107.24
Italy	25.48	United Kingdom	114.69
Canada	29.83	Hungary	134.96
Slovak Republic	32.66	Switzerland	151.58
USA	33.46	France	178.59
Ireland	53.39	Luxembourg	231.62
Sweden	67.13	Austria	239.81
Denmark	67.61		

Source: García-Posada and Mora-Sanguinetti (2012), "Why do Spanish firms rarely use the bankruptcy system?", The role of the mortgage institution, Documentos de trabajo, Banco de España-Eurosystem (forthcoming).

Lengthy procedures are likely to contribute to inefficiency. Bankruptcy cases took around 30 months to complete in 2010. While there are no international comparisons of the length of such procedures, civil justice procedures generally appear to be considerably longer in Spain than in most developed countries (see Mora-Sanguinetti and Fuentes, 2012 and references therein). While Spain has recently introduced specialised bankruptcy courts, a recent review of bankrupty procedures in Spain has argued that the system of appointments of the administrators for the firms filing for bankruptcy is deficient (Celentani et al., 2010). For example, the courts appear not to select administrators according to their expertise for a particular case.

The Spanish bankruptcy code implies higher expected costs of bankruptcy for managers than in most OECD countries. Unusually, it sets severe sanctions for a company manager for having caused or aggravated the firm's insolvency. There is no discharge for entrepreneurs. Moreover, Mora-Sanguinetti and Posada (2012) argue that inefficient bankruptcy procedures in Spain have encouraged creditors to use the mortgage system to secure their loans. These incentives appear to have been reinforced by the effectiveness of the mortgage system in protecting creditors. Such incentives may have biased business towards investing in assets which can serve as collateral, notably construction, to the detriment of investment in non-tangible capital, such as human capital and research. Unlike many OECD countries, Spain does not have discharge provisions, which allow entrepreneurs to make a "fresh start".

Bankruptcy procedures are rarely undertaken by households. In part, this is because most household debt consists of mortgage debt contracted with one bank, which enables both parties to negotiate debt restructuring without the framework of a formal bankruptcy procedure. However, Spanish households are subject to the same bankruptcy procedures as businesses, which are likely to be unnecessarily complex. Several OECD countries have introduced specific, simplified bankruptcy procedures for households, such as Germany or France, to facilitate access to such procedures. Moreover, as in the case of firms, according to Spanish legislation, the law does not provide for households to be discharged from their debt when exogenous economic circumstances of the household have changed such as to make repayment impossible.

The government took several measures in 2012 to encourage banks to offer discharge to over-indebted households voluntarily. It introduced a voluntary code which commits signatory banks to cancel the household's mortgage debt in exchange for the repossession of the home if no household member receives income from economic activity and if its non-housing assets are insufficient to repay any outstanding debt. Further conditions concerning the debt servicing burden of these households apply. Moreover, the minimum income which households cannot be obliged to use for debt-servicing was raised to 962 euros per month. Steps have also been taken to limit interest charges on overdue debt and improve the procedures for the auctioning of repossessed housing. Most banks have signed up to the code of conduct. For these banks the provisions of the code can be enforced by the courts. Nonetheless, a simplified bankruptcy regime, allowing a "fresh start" under well-defined restrictive conditions, could provide a broader framework for loss recognition and for avoiding unnecessary hardship, for example for households facing unsustainable consumer debt.

Box 1.9. Recommendations on deleveraging the private sector and overcoming the banking crisis

Improving housing policies

- Phase-out remaining tax advantages for residential housing, including preferential VAT rates for the sale of new housing and tax rebates on rental income as well as on realised capital gains.

- Shift the taxation of housing away from housing transactions towards the taxation of real estate values.

- Consider introducing an earmarked cash benefit towards the housing costs of poor households.

Strengthening the banking sector

- Viable banks in need of capital should be recapitalised promptly, as set out in the Memorandum of Understanding, addressing their potential credit losses in full, based on capital needs identified in independent assessments of individual bank balance sheets. Non-viable banks should be resolved in an orderly manner as soon as possible.

- The government guarantees for bank debt issuance should be phased out as soon as possible once the most solvent banks have regained access to wholesale funding markets.

- Holders of subordinated debt and lower-ranked hybrid capital instruments should absorb losses of banks that are resolved or are recapitalised by the government, as foreseen in the Memorandum of Understanding. Potential fiscal costs could be reduced further by imposing losses on senior debt, in addition to subordinated debt, for banks in orderly resolution procedures. Where consumer protection concerns exist, smaller losses should be imposed on retail investors.

- Consider introducing depositor preference in the hierarchy of creditors in the resolution of banks.

- Investigate consumer protection concerns with respect to the sale of subordinate debt to bank customers. Ensure liability of bank managers.

Box 1.9. **Recommendations on deleveraging the private sector and overcoming the banking crisis** (*cont.*)

- The authorities should be proactive in preventing any payouts or repurchases of capital when the capacity of loss-absorption is compromised. The supervisor should be given powers to prevent banks from repurchasing subordinate debt or carrying out other pay-outs if they reduce the availability of bank debt instruments to absorb losses.

- Contributions of the banking sector to fund remaining resolution costs should be separated from the contributions to deposit insurance and be assessed on the total of bank balance sheets.

- The supervisor should be given powers to claw back compensation payments of managers of banks which are resolved or recapitalised by government.

- Consider raising provisioning requirements on finished housing and valuing related exposures more closely according to market prices of underlying collateral.

- Impaired legacy assets transferred to the planned asset management company should be conservatively priced. Consider using debt that has been selected for loss absorption to help fund the transfer of assets from a bank to the asset management company.

Complete the reform of the savings banks

- Management of the banking subsidiaries should be kept at arms' length from their savings bank holdings.

- The independence of management of the savings banks from local political influence should be strengthened, for example by introducing fit-and-proper tests for all savings bank senior management.

Reform bankruptcy legislation

- Review bankruptcy proceedings for non-financial businesses to raise their efficiency. Take steps to accelerate judicial proceedings. Reduce the expected costs to managers by limiting the threat of sanctions and widening the applicability of debt discharge, for example with an automatic discharge after a set period of time (*e.g.* one year as in the UK).

- Consider introducing simplified bankruptcy procedures for households including the option of a "fresh start" under well-defined conditions.

Notes

1. Recent data on rented apartments are available for the region of Catalonia, where they increased by 30% between 2009 and 2011 (Generalitat de Catalunya, 2012).

2. No breakdown of lending statistics for the savings banks and other banks are available, as the distinction between savings banks and commercial banks has become blurred by reform of the corporate governance of savings banks. See for example the compilation of individual banks' account data in *El País* (2012).

3. Provisions were sourced from profits, general provisions and hidden reserves of merging banks.

4. "Principal capital" includes bonds which must be converted into equity by 2014 and which may not count as common equity under the *Basel III* rules. "Principal capital" also requires unrealised valuation losses to diminish capital even when it may not be required under *Basel III* losses.

5. The lower number applies. For banks majority-owned by the government a limit of 600 000 euros applies.

Bibliography

Ahrend, R. and A. Goujard (2011), "Drivers of Systemic Banking Crises: The Role of Bank-Balance-Sheet Contagion and Financial Account Structure", *OECD Economics Department Working Papers*, No. 902, OECD Publishing.

Andrews, D., A. Caldera Sánchez and Å. Johansson (2011), "Housing Markets and Structural Policies in OECD Countries", *OECD Economics Department Working Papers*, No. 836, OECD Publishing.

Angeloni, C. and G.B. Wolff (2012), "Are Banks Affected by their Holdings of Government Debt?", *Bruegel Working Paper*, No. 2012-07.

Aspachs-Bracons, O., J. Jódar-Rosell and J. Gual (2011), "Perspectivas de desapalancamiento en España", *Documentos de economía la Caixa*, No. 23.

Banco de España (2012a), *Annual Report*, Madrid.

Banco de España (2012b), *Financial Stability Report*, April, Madrid.

Banco de España (2012c), *Boletín Económico*, April, Madrid.

Bhutta, N. (2012), "Mortgage Debt and Household Deleveraging: Accounting for the Decline in Mortgage Debt Using Consumer Credit Record Data", Federal Reserve Board, March, mimeo, electronic copy available at: *http://ssrn.com/abstract=2027262*.

Bouis, R., B. Cournède and A.K. Christensen (2012), "Implications of Output Gap Uncertainty in Times of Crisis", *OECD Economics Department Working Papers*, No. 977.

Brown, M., A. Haughwout, D. Lee and W. van der Klaauw (2012), "Have Consumers Been Deleveraging?", *Federal Reserve Bank of New York*, Household Finance Blog, *http://ftalphaville.ft.com/blog/2011/03/21/521536/us-deleveraging-isnt-just-about-defaults-and-charge-offs/*.

Celentani, M., M. García-Posada and F. Gómez (2010), "The Spanish Business Bankruptcy Puzzle and the Crisis", *FEDEA Working Paper 2010-11*.

Davydenko, S.A. and J.R. Franks (2008), "Do Bankruptcy Codes Matter? A Study of Default in France, Germany, and the UK", *The Journal of Finance*, Vol. 52.

Financial Stability Board (FSB) (2011), "Key Attributes of Effective Resolution Regimes for Financial Institutions".

Fundación Fomento de Estudios Sociales y Socilogía Aplicada (FOESSA) (2008), VI. *Informe sobre desarrollo y exclusion social en España*.

García-Posada, M. and J.S. Mora-Sanguinetti (2012), "Why do Spanish firms rarely use the bankruptcy system?", The role of the mortgage institution, *Documentos de trabajo*, Banco de España-Eurosystem (forthcoming).

Generalitat de Catalunya (2012), "Informe continu sobre el sector de l'habitage a Catlunya », May 2012.

International Monetary Fund (IMF) (2002), "Building Strong Banks Through Surveillance and Resolution", Washington, DC.

IMF (2012a), *World Economic Outlook*, May 2012, Washington, DC.

IMF (2012b), "Spain: Financial Sector Stability Assessment", Washington, DC.

IMF (2012c), "Spain: Vulnerabilities of Private Sector Balance Sheets and Risks to the Financial Sector Technical Notes", *IMF Country Report*, No. 12/140, Washington, DC.

IMF (2012d), "Spain: The Reform of Spanish Savings Banks Technical Notes", *IMF Country Report*, No. 12/141, Washington, DC.

IMF (2012e), "From Bail-out to Bail-in: Mandatory Debt Restructuring of Systemic Financial Institutions", *IMF Staff Discussion Note*, April, Washington, DC.

Mora-Sanguinetti, J. and A. Fuentes (2012), "An Analysis of Productivity Performance in Spain Before and During the Crisis: Exploring the Role of Institutions", *OECD Economics Department Working Papers*, No. 973, Paris.

OECD (2007), *OECD Economic Surveys: Spain*, Paris.

OECD (2010), *OECD Economic Surveys: Spain*, Paris.

OECD (2011), *OECD Economic Surveys: Euro Area*, Paris.

Promontory (2012), "Independent Analysis of the Results and Methodology of the June 2012 Stress Test on the Spanish Banking System", Washington, DC.

World Bank (2002), "Bank Loan Classification and Provisioning Practices in Selected Developed and Emerging Countries", Finance Forum 2002.

Chapter 2

Improving employment prospects for young workers

The unemployment rate among young people has reached painfully high levels, in particular among those young people with low levels of education. There are two crucial policy priorities to improve employment prospects for youth in Spain. First, in the very short term, there is need for quick action to target well-designed active labour market programmes to the most disadvantaged youth and provide more job-search assistance and guidance for all youth experiencing difficulties in finding a job in the current labour market. Second, the current crisis is an opportunity to tackle some of the structural weaknesses in the Spanish youth labour market. This implies in particular reforms to prevent youth from dropping out of education at a very early stage and to improve the school to work transition of young people. Key issues are to better match skills acquired in education to those asked for by businesses, as well as to establish an effective system of vocational education, and to reduce remaining demand side barriers, notably labour market duality and a rigid collective bargaining system, which both have prevented an efficient allocation of labour resources in the past and a flexible adjustment during the crisis.

Labour market challenges

In Spain, youth employment rates rose from 1995 to 2007, reaching comparable levels to other OECD countries and higher than the average euro area country in 2007 (Figure 2.1, Panel A). Additional empirical evidence suggests that on average between 2000 and 2007, employment rates for 15-24 years old have been similar to countries with comparable labour market institutions such as France, but have been significantly lower than in other European countries, notably the Netherlands, with more liberal labour markets (Dolado *et al.*, 2012). Since 2007, the employment rate has fallen drastically (Figure 2.1, Panel A), losing the gains made during the boom period, and even beyond. While the youth unemployment rate among the 15-to-24-year-olds fell significantly between 1995 and 2007, it bottomed out at close to 20% even in the expansion period, and has doubled since 2007, reaching 45% in 2011 (Figure 2.1, Panel B). At the end of 2011, almost 70% of the 15 to 19 year olds in the labour force were without a job (INE, 2012).

Figure 2.1. Youth employment and unemployment performance has been poor

16 24 years old[1]

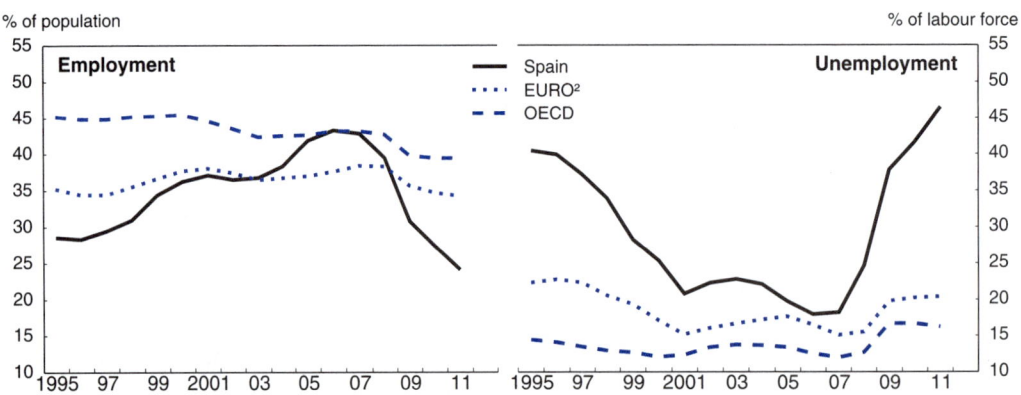

1. Age 15-24 for euro area and OECD.
2. Euro area 12 member countries prior to enlargement in 2007.
Source: OECD (2012), *Labour Force Statistics Database*, November.

StatLink ⟐ *http://dx.doi.org/10.1787/888932740499*

While youth unemployment is in all countries typically more sensitive to the cycle than that of prime age workers, this is particularly true in Spain. Empirical evidence suggests that in Spain, a 1 percentage point deviation of GDP growth from its potential would raise unemployment of youth by 2.3 percentage points, almost one percentage point more than youth unemployment in the OECD country on average (OECD, 2010a). During the recent crisis, unemployment of young people in Spain rose by 30 percentage points, as compared to 12 percentage points for adult workers, the highest increase among OECD countries (Figure 2.2). To a large extent this relates to the high prevalence of young people

Figure 2.2. **The increase in youth unemployment during the recent crisis has been particularly strong**

Percentage points difference from 2007-Q4 to 2011-Q4[1]

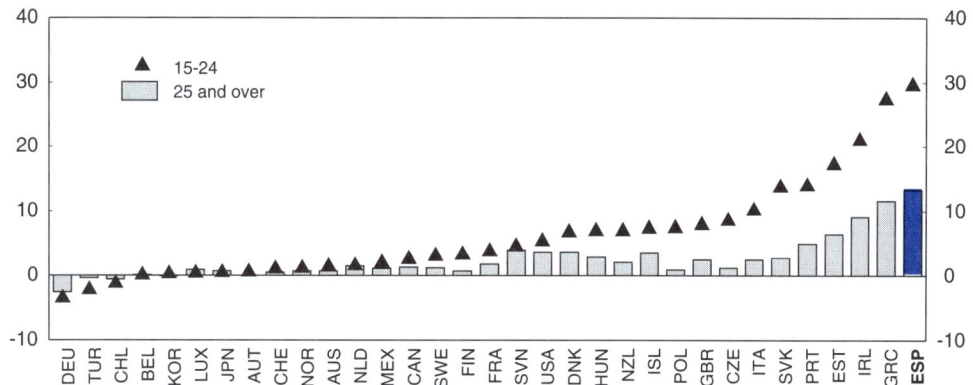

1. Data non seasonally adjusted for Chile, Iceland, Mexico, and Switzerland.
Source: OECD based on Eurostat, *Short-Term Indicators* and various national sources.

StatLink 🔗 *http://dx.doi.org/10.1787/888932740518*

on temporary contracts; in the past and in particular during the recent crisis, positive and negative employment growth has been mainly driven by creation and cuts of temporary jobs (OECD, 2010b).

Spain has one of the highest shares of the youth population who are neither in employment nor in education or training (NEET). There is a risk that these young people become excluded from the labour market. In the first quarter of 2011, about 20% of 15-24 years old youth have neither been in employment nor in education or training (Figure 2.3). This number is especially high and has more than doubled since 2007 for those young people who are between 20 and 24 years old (Dolado *et al.*, 2012). In contrast to most other OECD countries, the largest share of youth neither in employment nor in education or training are unemployed and not inactive. This can be explained by a high incidence of young people moving from one short-term temporary contract to another, frequently interspersed with unemployment spells.

Figure 2.3. **A large share of youth are not in employment and not in education or training (NEET)**

NEET rate, by status, as percentage of population aged 15/16-24, 2011-Q1

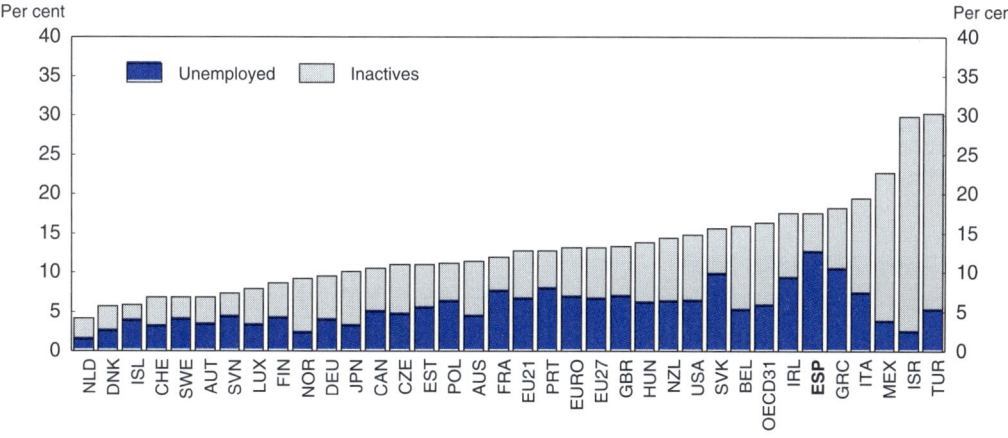

Source: OECD estimates based on *National Labour Force Surveys*.

StatLink 🔗 *http://dx.doi.org/10.1787/888932740537*

There are two crucial policy priorities to improve employment prospects for youth in Spain. *First,* in the very short term, new entrants into unemployment and those who already encountered difficulties in finding a job need to remain connected to the labour market. This implies quick action to provide job-search assistance and guidance for all youth experiencing difficulties in finding a job, and to target well designed active labour market programmes to the most disadvantaged youth. It also implies reinforcing the unemployment insurance system, coupled with strict enforcement of the requirements for unemployment benefit recipients to search and accept jobs, so as to avoid the high unemployment from becoming persistent.

Second, relatively high unemployment, even in the boom period, and the volatile reaction during the crisis indicate deep structural weaknesses in the youth labour market. The current crisis is an opportunity to tackle some of these weaknesses. In particular, reforms to prevent youth from dropping out of education at a very early stage are key to improving employability. Spain's skill-distribution is characterised by a very high share of youth having attained at most lower secondary education. In contrast to most other OECD countries, the unemployment rate of low-skilled workers was not much higher than that of skilled workers until 2007 (Figure 2.4, Panel A), reflecting abundant low-skilled jobs in the construction, hotels and restaurant, and tourism sectors in the past. However, these low-skilled youth were the first to lose their job during the crisis; unemployment of youth with at most lower secondary education almost tripled between 2007 and 2011 (Figure 2.4, Panel A), contributing the bulk to overall youth unemployed in 2011 (Figure 2.4, Panel B). Additional empirical evidence suggests that only a very small share of those unemployed continue education: in 2010, about 70% of 15-29 year old youth with at most lower secondary education have been neither in employment nor in education or training (NEET), between 20 to 30 percentage points higher than in other European countries (Dolado *et al.*, 2012).

Figure 2.4. **Unemployment is particularly high among low skilled youth**

Age group 15-24

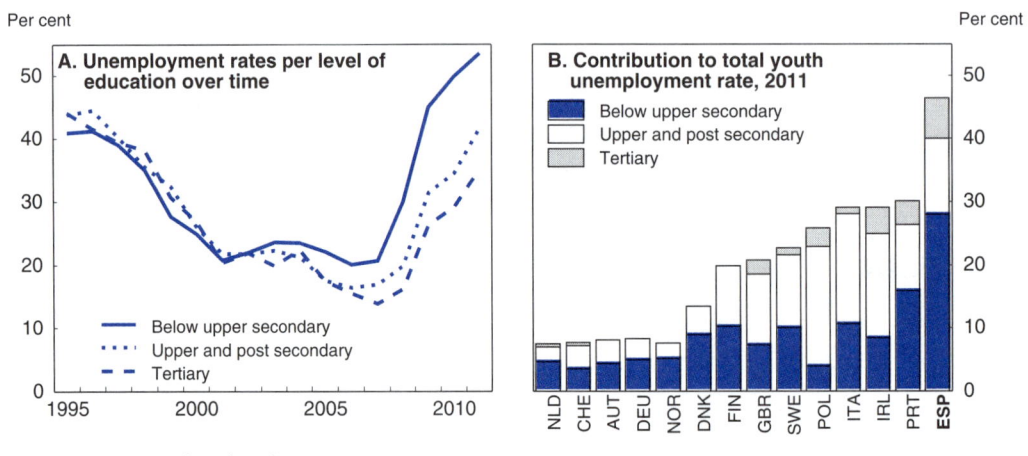

Source: *Eurostat Database* (2012), August.

StatLink ᴍ⫟ᴢ▸ *http://dx.doi.org/10.1787/888932740556*

Addressing crucial weakness in the Spanish youth labour market is also necessary to improve the employment prospects of young people in the long-term (Scarpetta *et al.*, 2010), notably as concerns the school to work transition. In Spain, the time required to find a first regular job of more than 3 months is significantly longer than in other European countries (Dolado *et al.*, 2012), and this has already been the case before the crisis. For instance, 2009 estimates suggest that 3 to 5 years after having left education (for the last time), almost 20% of the 15-34 years old had not found a job, compared to 5-6% in the Netherlands or the UK. And of those who had found a job 3 to 5 years after leaving education, it took them more than one year on average in Spain to find it, as compared to four months in the UK and six months in the Netherlands (Table 2.1). Issues to be dealt with in order to improve employment prospects of young people in Spain are to better match skills acquired in education and those asked for by businesses, to establish an effective system of vocational education that could smooth the transition from school to work, and to reduce remaining demand side barriers, notably labour market duality and a rigid collective bargaining system, which has prevented a flexible adjustment to the crisis and an efficient allocation of labour resources.

Table 2.1. **Time needed to find a job[1] since leaving school is long, 15-34 years old, 2009**

Months since leaving school	Percentage of 15-34 years old Who have not found a regular job				Average time needed to find a regular job, in months			
	Spain	France	Netherlands	United Kingdom	**Spain**	France	Netherlands	United Kingdom
13-24	**40.4**	25.5	6.1	10.7	**4.1**	3.7	2.1	3.1
25-36	**28.1**	17.3	5.4	8.3	**6.3**	6.2	3.6	4.2
37-48	**18.5**	12.9	5.8	8.1	**9.3**	5.7	5.2	4.3
49-60	**19.7**	15.4	5.0	4.3	**12.8**	6.7	6.3	4.4

1. The average time needed to find a regular job applies to those who have found a job at the time of the interview.
Source: Dolado *et al.* (2012), based on 2009 *EU Labour Force Survey ad hoc* module.

In 2012, the government introduced a package of wide-ranging labour market measures to address these challenges. The measures were introduced in February and took effect immediately; after having been slightly amended, the law has been in force since July 2012. In general, these reforms are a substantial step in the right direction. While it is still too early to assess the impact of the reform, there are areas where they need to be complemented and made more effective, as described below.

In the short term, ensure that youth-at-risk remain connected to the labour market

There is need for better targeted active labour market policies

In the short term, well targeted and well designed active labour market policies (ALMP) help ensure that school leavers and young unemployed do not risk being excluded from the labour market (OECD, 2010a, Scarpetta *et al.*, 2010). This is especially important for Spain given the large share of young people who are neither in employment nor in education or training (Figure 2.3). In this context, measures that have proven most effective are job-search assistance and guidance for all young people experiencing difficulties in finding a job, as well as obligatory training measures (OECD, 2010a; Scarpetta *et al.*, 2010).

While participation in active labour market policies (ALMP) is high in Spain as compared to other countries, ALMPs consist to a very large extent in employment incentives, mainly in the form of subsidies to firms hiring on permanent contracts (Figure 2.5). While a wide range

Figure 2.5. **Participation in activation is poor – even during the crisis**[1]

Young participants aged 15-24 in active measures, as a percentage of the youth labour force, 2008

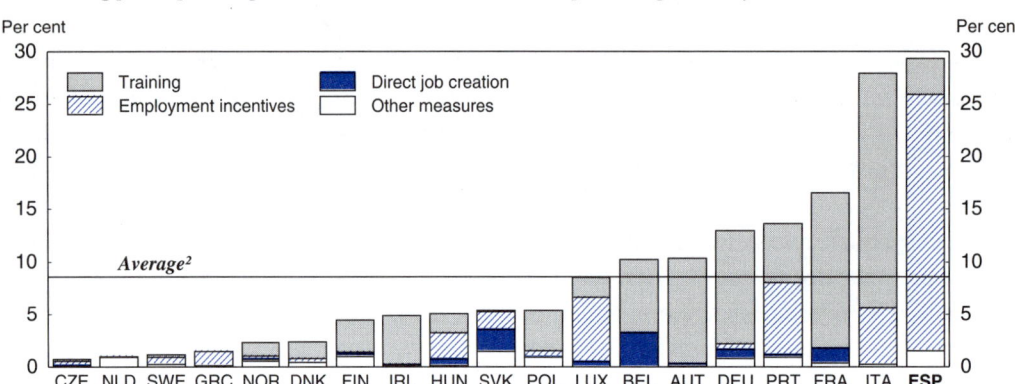

1. Data cover at least 80% of the participants in active labour market measures(categories from 2 to 7 of Eurostat and OECD nomenclature).
2. Unweighted average of countries shown.
Source: OECD (2010), *Off to a Good Start? Jobs for Youth.*

StatLink ᗰᔐᑏ *http://dx.doi.org/10.1787/888932740575*

of hiring subsidies were abolished in 2012, new subsidies have been introduced. These include in particular financial incentives for firms with fewer than 50 employees to hire young people below 30 years old on permanent employment contracts (Box 2.1).

Subsidies to private-sector jobs may enhance effective labour supply by helping individuals to keep in contact with work, thereby maintaining their motivation and skills. The experience from previous downturns has shown that under conditions of very weak labour demand, such incentives can jump-start job creation, in particular if targeted on vulnerable groups (De Serres *et al.*, 2012; Scarpetta *et al.*, 2010). However, the subsidies for hiring youth and long-term unemployed on permanent contracts should only be used as a temporary instrument during the recession; post-recession they should be phased out – as is being done for most hiring subsidies. In any case they should be targeted solely on the most disadvantaged or difficult to place youth. Empirical evidence suggests that subsidies can have large deadweight losses and substitution effects and as a result, most such schemes yield small net employment gains. For instance, evaluations of wage subsidies in Australia, Belgium, Ireland and the Netherlands have suggested combined deadweight and substitution effects amounting to around 90%, implying that for every subsidised 100 jobs only ten were net gains in terms of employment (Martin and Grubb, 2001). Hiring subsidies have also proven largely ineffective in Spain, and at the same time have been very costly for public finances (OECD, 2010b).

Fully phasing out of hiring subsidies is particularly important in the case of the new permanent contract for firms with less than 50 employees. On top of deadweight losses, this contract risks increasing excess turnover and raising unemployment. The contract foresees an extended trial period of one year, in which the worker has no right to receive severance pay on dismissal, and subsidies are paid for the first three years of the contract. Even if firms that terminate the contract before the three years would have to repay the subsidies, the contract may act as another form of temporary contract with very low firing costs as long as firms hire an employee and fire him within the trial period. The new contract will be valid as

> ### Box 2.1. **Active labour market policies in the 2012 labour market reform**
>
> The 2012 labour market reform increases employment incentives and aims to improve the matching of people to jobs in the following ways:
>
> *First,* it introduces new financial incentives for firms hiring young unemployed people. In particular, it introduces a new permanent contract for firms with less than 50 employees; this new contract is temporary and will be valid as long as the unemployment rate is above 15% (see also Box 2.4).
>
> ● If firms hire a long-term unemployed worker (having received unemployment benefits for at least three months) on this contract, they are entitled to a one-off tax deduction of 3 000 euros and during 12 months, a tax deduction of 50% of the unemployment benefits which the newly hired worker would have received at the time of hiring. The newly hired worker will be entitled to receive 25% of their remaining unemployment benefit entitlement on top of their wage.
>
> ● If firms hire young unemployed workers between 16 and 30 years old on the new contract, they are entitled to rebates on employers' social security contributions during three years. The rebates would amount to 1 000 euros/year in the first year, 1 100 euros/year in the second year and 1 200 euros/year in the third year.
>
> ● Hiring on the new contract is subject to a trial period of one year during which the workers are not entitled to severance payments. In the case of dismissal before three years, the firm has to repay the financial incentives received.
>
> *Second,* young people below 30 can now use up to 100% of their accumulated unemployment benefits if they opt to capitalise their benefits to start up an enterprise.
>
> *Third,* the system of on-the-job training and training of unemployed workers is being transformed through the introduction of a voucher (cuenta formación), recentralisation of the training priorities and introducing competition in the selection of training providers.
>
> *Fourth,* temporary employment and private employment agencies can now provide placement without the formal requirements that were established in the reform of 2010.
>
> *Finally,* the conditionality and the obligation to take on a suitable job was increased for unemployed workers who have used up their first tier unemployment benefit. And the unemployment insurance benefit replacement ratio was reduced to 50% from the 7th month of the unemployment spell onwards. Further, the means for the public employment service to supervise recipients, update their status and take actions accordingly have been reinforced.

long as the unemployment rate is above 15%. This goes in the right direction, but it may take some time, even with the implementation of reform measures, before unemployment can be brought down by 10 percentage points from 25% in October 2012.

Increasing job-search assistance would help young people experiencing difficulties in finding a job. These measures have proven effective in other countries (OECD, 2010a). In a recession, the lower opportunity cost of time spent on training makes also training measures especially opportune (OECD, 2010c). Moreover, training would help the unemployed acquire a different set of skills so as to prepare them for a job outside their previous occupation. This is particularly important for Spain where the economic recovery is likely to require significant structural change. Some steps are being introduced in this direction (Box 2.1). This is welcome, but more is likely to be needed.

The mutual obligation system of unemployment insurance has to be reinforced

While the unemployment benefit system in Spain has played a significant role in supporting the growing number of unemployed during the crisis, rising long-term unemployment has lowered coverage of unemployment insurance benefits. Hence, active labour market policies and re-employment services to the unemployed need to be made more effective, coupled with strict enforcement of the requirements for unemployment benefit recipients to search for and accept jobs, so as to reduce unemployment and avoid it from becoming persistent (De Serres et al., 2012).

The 2012 labour market reform allows for-profit temporary employment agencies to act as private placement agencies under contract to the public employment service. This is welcome, as with the surge in unemployment during the recent crisis regional public employment services may better concentrate on particular target groups and "outsource" other activities. Further initiatives will be needed, however, given the scale of the problem.

First, the division between the financing of unemployment benefits with unemployment insurance contributions at the national level, on the one hand, and the managing of the placement services at the regional level, on the other hand, may distort placement incentives for regional employment offices (OECD, 2008, 2010b). Regions do not receive the fiscal benefits of a reduction in unemployment. Rather, as resources are allocated across regions according to the number of unemployed, regions that succeed in placing the unemployed receive less funding. Moreover, there is a risk that ALMPs are not designed to promote employability, but to place recipients in short-term jobs that re-qualify them for unemployment benefits paid by the central government. The government may consider assigning the responsibilities for funding unemployment benefits and for managing the public employment services at the same jurisdictional level (the central government). The government has taken some steps towards monitoring and evaluation of placement services and ALMP implementation at regional level, based on quantitative output indicators (OECD, 2010b). This is welcome as such initiatives could help to improve incentives for regional employment services. Monitoring would best be combined with a stronger co-ordination among regional placement services so as to exchange best practices.

Second, the Spanish mutual obligation approach where, in return for benefits, recipients are required to engage in active job search activities, could be better enforced, in line with recommendations in earlier OECD Economic Surveys (OECD, 2008, 2010b). Some steps have been taken to make progress (Box 2.1), which should be complemented. In particular, entitlement to unemployment benefits should start from the initial time of registration and should no longer be paid retroactively from registration (OECD, 2008). The first intensive placement interview should be mandatory at the time of registration and the frequency of interviews between the job-seekers and the employment counsellors should be increased so as to increase the opportunities of referral to a vacancy. The requirements for unemployed to take on a "suitable" job should be reinforced early on in the unemployment spell.

In the longer term, the government may also consider reducing the duration of unemployment benefits which with a maximum of about two years is relatively long. By reducing the job-search intensity of the unemployed, a generous level or long duration of unemployment benefits can result in longer periods of unemployment. Arellano et al. (1998), for instance, based on longitudinal hazard estimations for a sample of Spanish men in 1987-94, show that receipt of unemployment benefits significantly reduces the probability of leaving unemployment. Furthermore, by lowering the opportunity cost of not working, they may also put upward pressure on workers' wage claims and ultimately reduce labour demand (OECD, 2006). The government reduced the replacement ratio after the 7 months of the unemployment spell from 60 to 50%. Empirical studies have found that long benefit duration is more detrimental to employment than high replacement rates (OECD, 2006). Shortening the duration of benefits may also not hit those unemployed who would need them most. People on temporary contracts have a higher probability of job loss, yet may accumulate little benefit entitlement, while people on permanent contracts would be entitled to generous unemployment benefits in case of a dismissal in addition to high severance pay (OECD, 2010b).[1]

Reducing the early drop-out rate from education

The share of low skilled among young unemployed has been particularly high in Spain in international comparison, and increased drastically since 2007. These facts point to possible weaknesses in the education system. Spain's educational distribution is characterised by a particularly high share of youth in the 15-29 year age bracket who leave school with at most lower secondary education (OECD, 2010). While the share of the population who have obtained the certificate of obligatory (lower) secondary education has increased from 71% in 2007 to about 74% in 2010, this is very low in international comparison (MECD, 2012). Only 48% of young people graduate from general upper secondary education (Figure 2.6, Panel A) and while access to and graduation from tertiary education has increased over the past ten years (OECD, 2008), the number of graduates from tertiary education is still low in international comparison (Figure 2.6, Panel B). There are two main areas to address:

Figure 2.6. **Graduation from upper secondary and tertiary education is weak**
In per cent of the population at the typical graduation age,[1] 2010

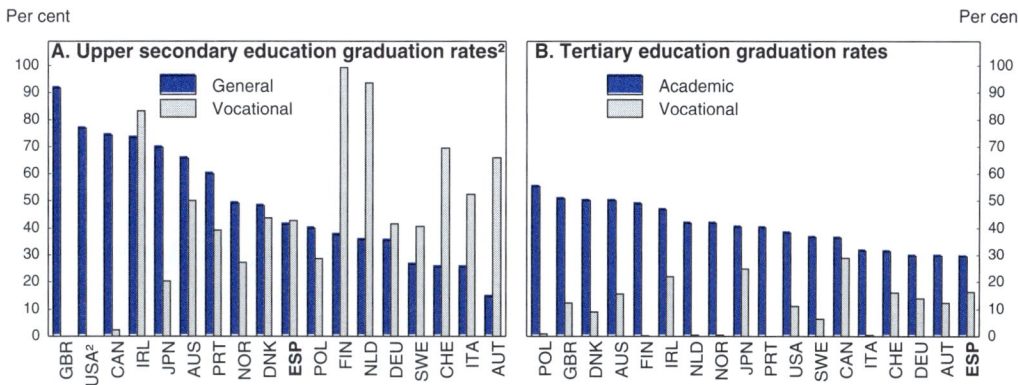

1. Graduation rates measure the estimated percentage of young adults who graduate from this level of education during their lifetimes.
2. Total upper secondary education.
Source: OECD (2012), *Education at a Glance.*

StatLink ⬛ http://dx.doi.org/10.1787/888932740594

First, in Spain, a large number of pupils repeat grades; some fail lower secondary education. In 2009, 35% of 15 year olds had repeated a grade at least once in Spain as compared to an average of 13% in all OECD countries (OECD, 2011a; OECD, 2008). Grade repetition is ineffective in raising educational outcomes (OECD, 2012a). Still, teachers and society support this practice, and there is not much awareness of the long-term negative effects on students. In fact, the chances for those young people of finding a job at a later stage are very weak, and passing lower secondary education is the main entry into higher level education also at a later stage of life (García-Perez *et al.*, 2011; OECD, 2008). Those who repeat are often from disadvantaged backgrounds and this contributes to widen inequities. Grade repetition also creates large costs for society as a whole, including the expense of providing an additional year of education for a student, and the cost to society of delaying that student's entry into the labour market by at least one year. PISA estimates suggest that the cost of using grade repetition for one age group in Spain is equivalent to at least 10% of annual national expenditure on primary and secondary school education (OECD, 2011a).[2]

One reason for the high grade repetition rate in Spain is the relatively stringent requirements to pass the certificate of compulsory (lower) secondary education (GESO). Students move to the subsequent grade if they have failed at most two subjects. In the final year, students have to pass everything eventually, although there are second-round exams for those who fail some subjects. Students can repeat a grade twice at most, and if they reach the age of 16 without having passed the GESO, their parents can decide to take them out of education (MECD, 2012). Moreover, there are few incentives for schools and teachers to reduce repetition, as individual schools are funded based on the number of students enrolled and do not have to internalise these costs, and alternatives such as personalised learning or targeted interventions often have direct costs for schools.

The government is planning to reform the education system so as to raise educational outcomes, and in particular reduce grade repetition and the high drop-out rate from lower secondary education. The government plans to strengthen the core subjects necessary to acquire basic skills to follow any level of upper secondary education by reducing the overall number of competencies and putting more weight in terms of hours taught on the core subjects, mathematics, language and science. Strengthening the core subjects is welcome. However, there is the risk that this measure will not reduce grade repetition unless coupled with less stringent conditions for grade advancement. The criteria for granting pupils' promotion to subsequent grades, and hence access to upper secondary education, should be focused more closely on these competencies that are instrumental for following any type of upper secondary education, as was recommended in past *OECD Economic Surveys*. This would reduce grade repetition in compulsory secondary education more effectively, and could be introduced quickly.

This could be coupled with a stronger focus on measures to prevent repetition, by addressing learning gaps during the school year, while reducing grade repetition substantially to few exceptional cases (OECD, 2012a). The government plans to address this issue to some extent through improved autonomy of the schools along with the introduction of the external and standardised tests. This would include external tests at the end of each education level (primary school, compulsory secondary school and upper secondary education) as well as a test in the 3rd year of primary school, aimed at the early detection of learning problems. Students passing this external test at the end of lower secondary school will be granted the final certification and can move to upper secondary level, provided they fail in at most two subjects.

The government also wants to allow students to follow a vocational track already in the final year of compulsory education, so as to reduce drop out from lower secondary education and make vocational education more attractive. It is planned that some core subjects would remain the same in both tracks with students sharing the courses. The two tracks would lead to different degrees which provide different access opportunities in upper secondary education. There is a risk that this may increase dependence of student performance on family background and reduce equality of opportunity. Moreover, it may also not reduce grade repetition as it would apply only to those students in the final year of lower secondary education, when grade repetition has already occurred in many cases. Maintaining education pathways open and equivalent for all pupils completing lower secondary education could help improve equal opportunities (OECD, 2012a).

Second, staying in education has not been the preferred option for many students as the skill premium of upper secondary education and tertiary education was relatively low in terms of lower gross earnings gains and weaker career prospects over an individual's working life than in other countries (OECD, 2011b). University fees were lower than on average across OECD countries in 2008-09 (latest comparable OECD data available, OECD, 2012c) although they have risen since. Access to public loans for students is limited to postgraduate courses. Furthermore, support to students enrolled in tertiary education as a share of public expenditure in tertiary education is relatively low in Spain as compared to other European countries (Eurydice, 2012). Access to higher education, especially tertiary education, has been particularly difficult for qualified students from more disadvantaged families. Conditions to grants for students from poor families have been tightened by introducing a stricter link between grants and academic results, and scholarships offered are not sufficient to cover costs of living (OECD, 2009a; Eurydice, 2012). A programme of loans with income-contingent repayments for tertiary education and improved access to grants for students from socially disadvantaged families could address this weakness (OECD, 2008).

Facilitating the transition from school to work through improved vocational education

The school-to-work transition of young people is typically smoother in countries with well developed vocational education by providing work-related skills through curricula which emphasise the acquisition of practical skills that are relevant for work (OECD, 2010d). Moreover, vocational education allows for an alternative track for youth disaffected with academic education and at high risk of dropping out. However, in Spain, graduation rates from upper secondary vocational education are very low, reflecting weak incentives for young people to follow a vocational stream as compared to either staying in general education or entering the labour market immediately after lower secondary education (Figure 2.7). In 2009, about 45% of young people in the typical age of upper secondary education were enrolled in vocational education programmes in Spain, as compared to about 70% in Switzerland. And of those students who are enrolled in vocational upper secondary education, only very few participate in programmes in which school- and work-based training is combined, as compared to Germany or Switzerland, where combined (dual) vocational education is frequent (Figure 2.7).

Weaknesses of the system in place

There are four main weaknesses in the Spanish vocational education system that would have to be addressed to improve its attractiveness and its efficiency. *First,* combined vocational programmes are most effective in facilitating the transition from school to work (OECD, 2010d). However, in Spain, vocational education programmes lack a proper combination between formal school and work-based education; workplace based training

Figure 2.7. **Combined school and work-based programmes
of vocational education are rare**

Enrolment in upper secondary vocational programmes in all programmes (total) and in those programmes
in which school-and work-based training is combined, 2010, in per cent of the typical age of population

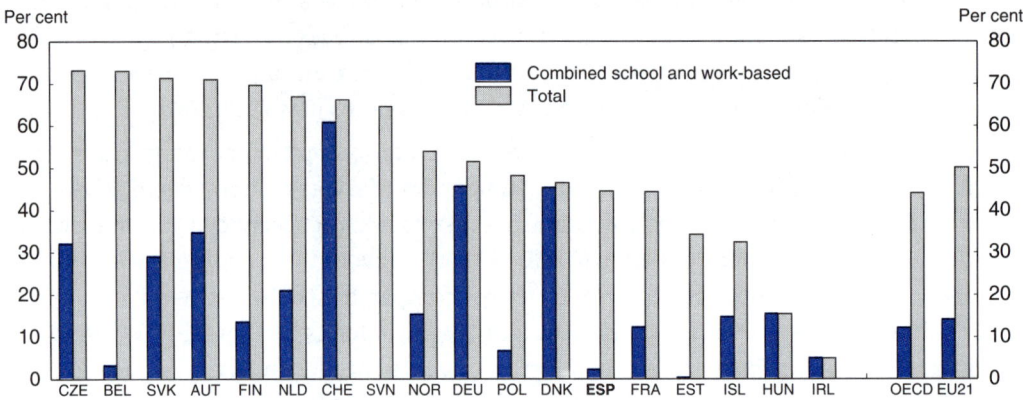

Source: OECD (2012), *Education at a Glance.*

StatLink ⎯⎯ http://dx.doi.org/10.1787/888932740613

typically takes place for a very short period of time (up to at most 20% of total vocational programmes) and only at the very end of the two years of the programme, preventing young people from gaining an early appreciation and understanding of the world of work.

Second, while the aim of vocational education is to prepare students for the labour market, the content of vocational education in Spain appears not to meet labour market needs. For instance, there is no requirement for vocational education teachers and trainers to have worked in their vocational field (OECD, 2012b) and courses in formal and vocational upper secondary schools are typically taught by the same teachers (MTI, 2008). Moreover, it appears that firms have had only limited influence on the curricula, further lowering the relevance of vocational programmes for firms. Employers are involved in the general curricula of the vocational education system through the General Council for Vocational Education at the national level, which aims to build consensus among the national and autonomous community governments, and employers and unions, on vocational education policy. However, *de facto* at the local level, employers are engaged in the system particularly through the provision of workplace training, which has not been a very substantial part of overall vocational education (MTI, 2008; OECD, 2012b). Hence, for the firm it may be more profitable to hire a graduate from general upper secondary education who may be assumed to be more talented and hence more productive.[3]

Third, vocational education in Spain is purely publicly financed. It would be more efficient if the cost of vocational education were shared between government, employers and students according to the benefits obtained (OECD, 2010d). The positive social net returns from the investment in vocational education, due to positive effects for society as whole, justify public investment in vocational education. Moreover, to the extent that vocational education provides transferable skills, employers' incentives to share the costs are weakened, as they would lose their investment if the trainee left to another firm after the training. However, within a system in which formal school and workplace training is combined, the skills acquired at work are to some extent firm-specific, and firms can draw benefits from the training (see Box 2.2). Both effects justify contributions by firms to the funding, for instance by paying trainees a wage at least for the period of work-based training (Box 2.2, Wolter and Ryan, 2011; Höckel, 2008). Trainees would accept a lower wage in exchange to the skills acquired.

Box 2.2. **What makes firms invest in apprenticeship training?**

Empirical evidence suggests that a firm's willingness to train apprentices is a crucial condition for a successful vocational education system in which school-based and work-based training are combined (Wolter and Ryan, 2011). Firms do have an incentive to train young people, although the reasons and returns from apprenticeship training vary across occupations and across countries (Mohrenweiser and Zwick, 2009, Wolter and Ryan, 2011).

Investment in human capital differs from those in physical capital in that the firm does not acquire a property right over its investment in skills, so the firm and the worker have to share the costs and benefits of the investment. The question of who bears the costs of training within an apprenticeship or a dual vocational programme depends on the type of human capital acquired (Wolter and Ryan, 2011): if the skills are truly general (*i.e.* transferable across firms), the firm would not have an incentive to bear the costs of the training. In the absence of an enforceable contract, the firm would lose all its investment if the worker were to leave the training company. In this case, the worker who has an incentive to take up the training as the skills are transferable would bear the costs. If the training is purely firm-specific, neither the firm nor the trainee would have an incentive to finance all of the costs. Both parties would lose all their investment in the event of separation after the training. In this case, training would only take place under a sharing of the costs between the firm and the worker.

An apprenticeship system that includes both school-based and work-based training and that leads to recognised formal qualifications, ensures that firms provide training (and trainees take up the training) although the apprenticeship provides at least to some extent transferable skills (Wolter and Ryan, 2011). Apprentices are mostly young people living with their parents, and are hence willing to accept a lower wage during the training in exchange of the skill acquired. Moreover, an apprenticeship contract commits the trainee to stay until its completion, as only then he/she would obtain the recognised qualification.

Empirical evidence suggests that the incentives for firms' investment in training are reinforced through the existence of market distortions or externalities (Wolter and Ryan, 2011):

● *Information asymmetries*: these mean that the wage paid in the external market will be lower than the true productivity of the ex-trainee, giving the training firm a competitive advantage in setting the post-training wage and increasing the incentive for the trainee to stay.

● *Industry- or occupation-specific monopsonies*: even if the skills acquired through an apprenticeship are transferable, they are still specific to an occupation or industry, reducing the number of firms that compete for a particular set of skills and raising the costs of changing jobs.

● *Skill complementarity*: firms may be willing to invest in general/transferable skills, as acquiring firm-specific skills is more productive if accompanied by the acquisition of general skills.

● *Make-or-buy*: by hiring former apprentices a firm can save on adaption costs that would arise by hiring skilled workers externally (Mohrenweiser and Zwick, 2009).

● *Labour market regulation*: apprenticeships can be used as a screening device to reduce the risk of a bad match and hence to reduce possible dismissal costs. Empirical evidence suggests for instance, that firms are willing to incur net costs in the short run to avoid costs implied by strong employment protection (Muehlemann *et al.*, 2010).

Fourth, so-called training contracts (*contratos de formacíon*)[4] aim to provide work-based training. However, the incentives for firms to offer such contracts on the one hand, and for young people to take on training contracts on the other hand, have been weak. The skills acquired through training contracts were not formally recognised, making young people reluctant to take on such jobs (OECD, 2007). Moreover, training contracts were typically relatively short and with a maximum duration of two years (OECD, 2007). Empirical evidence from apprenticeships system in Germany and Switzerland suggest that firms typically draw a net return from the training only in the second half of the apprenticeship, once the trainee can work with almost full productivity. In some cases this is only once the trainee has been taken over after the apprenticeship (Wolter and Ryan, 2011; Mohrenweiser and Zwick, 2009).

Towards an effective combined (dual) system of vocational education

The government is planning to reform the current vocational education system. It is envisaged to improve the existing components, the formal vocational programmes on the one hand and the training contracts on the other hand, to move towards a system combining formal school with longer work-based training (Box 2.3).

Box 2.3. **2012 reforms related to vocational education**

The government has prepared a draft Royal Decree to reform the existing system of vocational education and the training contracts (*contratos de formación*) to better tailor vocational education to the skill needs in the labor market, and to improve access to upper secondary education, reduce early school drop – out and facilitate the school-to-work transition. The reform seeks to achieve this in two ways:

First, it has improved the design of training contracts. Training contracts will be extended to a maximum of three years (as compared to two years now). If undertaken in an accredited firm, the training provided within a training contract is certified as a part of the educational qualification. Training will occupy at least one third (as compared to 15% now) and no more than 75% of the overall duration of the training contract. Trainees will receive a wage which cannot be lower than the minimum wage, though. Companies may receive public funds to cover part of the training costs, through rebates in employer contributions to Social Security. The Public Employment Service would manage the funds.

Second, the government is working with autonomous regions that have launched a set of pilot projects for a dual vocational education programme. Training could be provided exclusively within an accredited training center (educational body), exclusively in an authorised training company, or in co-operation between the two, where the firm would provide at least one third of the training. Students would either receive a wage from the firm or a grant from the educational institution, administered by the Public Employment Service.

These measures go in the right direction. However, the government should combine formal vocational education and training contracts within one single system. Training contracts should be extended for the whole period in which formal education takes place. In this way, work-based training would be on a continuous basis and would alternate with school based training, either some days per week or in blocks in regular intervals. As is envisaged, contracts would be signed between the trainee, the training firms and the representative for vocational education, respectively the vocational school, so as to increase commitment (see Box 2.2). By linking the content of the work-based training to the formal skills acquired at schools more closely, the combination of school-based vocational education and the training contracts would ensure that content in work-based training is in line with the requirements for a certain job and formally recognised. Finally, by combining school-based vocational education with training contracts, training firms pay a wage for work-based training and hence participate to the financing of the system, while the government can concentrate its contribution to the financing and provision of school-based training.

The government plans to provide firms offering a training contract with rebates of social security contributions (Box 2.2). However, there is a risk that firms abuse training contracts as a cheap way to hire trainees to do low-skilled jobs while providing only a minimum amount of training limited to what would be paid through subsidies. The incentives of the firms to offer training contracts and to participate in an apprenticeship programme would be best achieved by allowing them to pay the trainee, during the work-based training, a wage that can be lower than the minimum wage (OECD, 2007). While in aggregate the minimum wage is relatively low in Spain as compared to other countries, there are reasons to assume that it may often be high as compared to the median wage of young workers (see below).

Firms also need to be involved more widely in the curriculum of school-based training, as appears to be planned. Beyond improving the attractiveness of vocational education for firms, this would help ensure that curricula can be adapted to the rapidly changing nature of jobs, e.g. linked to the technical developments in information and communication. In Norway for instance, placing students in apprenticeships is achieved through Training Offices for Vocational Training at the local level, in which those firms co-operate which have common needs for trained workers or have decided to offer apprenticeships together. Municipal school authorities have a secretariat that provides support and help in establishing and running the circles. In addition, there are teachers in most schools who maintain contacts with enterprises as a regular part of their job (Kuczera et al., 2008). Consideration should also be given to opening up the teaching profession in vocational schools to practitioners more widely, which could raise the awareness of general teaching staff of ongoing developments (OECD, 2008).

Maintaining quality standards, both as regards teaching at school and training at the firm is a potential challenge. Some firms, notably small firms, may find it difficult to provide a combined vocational training, for instance because they are too specialised or lack the necessary professional infrastructure or technical equipment to cover all required areas of the particular training. Countries have come up with different ways to deal with this issue. In Germany, for instance, an individual firm can provide apprenticeships in co-operation with either another company or with an official training provider or educational institution (for instance a regional training center). This allows individual firms to share administrative and organisational costs or to offer specific elements or steps of the training for a particular occupation (BfA, 2012).

Finally, quality assessment mechanisms need to be in place, both at the level of the educational bodies or training centres that provide school-based training and at the firm level. Assessment should be based on general quantitative criteria based on the success of the training in moving graduates into suitable jobs (OECD, 2008). Setting up a system of indicators and analysis relating to vocational schools could be a starting point for more widespread evaluation of apprenticeship programmes. This could include the collection of data on the flow of students through education and on the long-term labour market performance of young people with a vocational degree (OECD, 2010d).

Ensuring that students leave education with skills asked for in the labour market

Educational qualification do not match skills requested by firms

In Spain, the prospects for young people to gain access to occupations that reflect the skills they have acquired in education are poor (OECD, 2008). This phenomenon is particularly prevalent for tertiary education graduates. About 40% of young people between 25 and 34 years old with a tertiary education degree are not employed in occupations that typically require this qualification, such as managers and professionals or technicians and associate professionals (Figure 2.8). In Spain, tertiary education graduates also need a long time to find a job, even on a temporary basis, and the average time needed to find a longer-term job of at least 3 months is 7 months in Spain as compared to 3 months in the United Kingdom and the Netherlands and 4.6 months in France (Eurydice, 2012). Moreover, a high rate of over-qualification has been observed already in the past and it has not changed much over the past decade (Eurydice, 2012). These facts point to distortions in the labour market, such as informational barriers in job search and lack of geographical or job mobility which avoid an efficient allocation of labour or skills resources to jobs (OECD, 2008; OECD, 2011c). In fact, once corrected for the incidence of temporary contracts, Spain shows a very low rate of job mobility, even within industries (OECD 2009b).

Figure 2.8. **Tertiary education graduates are employed in lower qualification jobs**

Distribution of people with tertiary education, aged 25-34, by occupational class, 2010, in percentage

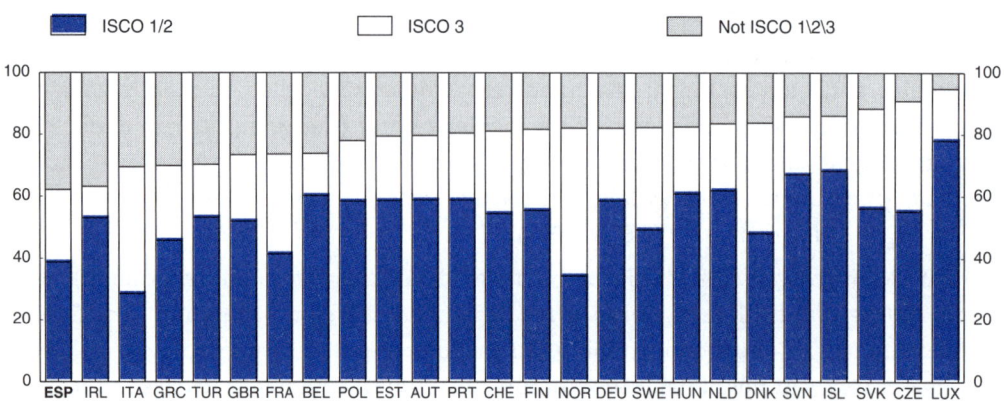

Note: ISCO 1/2: legislators, senior officials, managers and professionals; ISCO 3: technicians and associate professionals.
Source: Euridyce (2012).

StatLink 🔗 http://dx.doi.org/10.1787/888932740632

The high incidence of temporary employment and the lack of geographic and job mobility are to a large extent due to employment protection legislation, which has strongly favoured insiders on permanent contracts, and to a rigid collective bargaining system. Both have made it difficult or costly for firms to upgrade job content, open positions and hire workers with more appropriate skills. And employees on permanent contracts have had no incentive to move to another job, opening their position to younger people, as they risk losing their protection. As a consequence, young people move from one very short term temporary contract to the next before finding a longer term job, interspersed with frequent unemployment spells, with adverse effects for their longer term employability. The likelihood of a person being employed on a job for which she is over-qualified increases with the time spent in unemployment (OECD, 2011c). Addressing these weaknesses as described in the following sections would limit the adverse effects for the recovery and facilitate the switch to more export-led growth, beyond their positive effects on employment. Theoretical and empirical evidence suggests that the reallocation of labour resources to more productive uses is facilitated by on-the-job search and direct job-to-job transitions, rather than movements of workers through unemployment spells (Krause and Lubik, 2007).

Lack of geographical mobility is also driven by a housing market that favours home-ownership vis-à-vis the rental market. Linked to the low rate of conversion of temporary contracts into permanent ones, young workers face a high degree of uncertainty as to how long they will be able to remain in the same job or enterprise. It is also more difficult for young people to buy an apartment due to the limited availability of security they could provide so as to have access to a mortgage. Hence, young people may prefer to search and accept a job close to their families. In fact, empirical evidence suggests that in Spain, young people stay much longer with their parents than in other countries (Dolado *et al.*, 2012). Disincentives for renting should be reduced as described in Chapter 1.

On top of demand side barriers, inefficiencies in the education system need to be addressed

Addressing inefficiencies in the tertiary education system would help to ensure that the skills acquired in academic or vocational education match those demanded by the labour market. In fact, empirical evidence suggests that in Spain, a large share of workers are holding jobs in areas that are unrelated to their field of study (OECD, 2011c).

The following weaknesses should be addressed in particular:

- *First*, tertiary education curricula and programmes do not respond to the needs of the labour market (OECD, 2009a). Involving labour market actors, such as businesses, professions, and labour unions, in bodies that provide advice and analysis to educational policy authorities can help, as is the case already with employers' involvement in the General Council for Vocational Education. Public authorities should seek to widen participation of labour market actors also in the governing councils of tertiary education institutions.

- *Second*, academic tracks are favoured vis-à-vis vocational tracks, reducing the responsiveness of the educational system to labour market needs. Higher vocational or specialised tertiary education are disconnected from the tertiary education system, as they are seen instead as an extension of upper secondary education schools. This reduces their attractiveness and recognition as education of equal standard to academic tertiary education (OECD, 2009a). Higher vocational education should be integrated into the tertiary education system.

- *Third*, educational efficiency is weak, as reflected in a low number of students completing their studies in a given year when compared to total enrolments, and in a long time to completion. Indeed, the long time needed for completion appears to be taken by some teachers as a reflection of the "quality" of the programme (OECD, 2009a). Authorities should help the institutions improve their understanding of the longer-term career paths of graduates, for instance through the establishment and maintenance of a database that tracks graduates' labour market performance (OECD, 2009a). Besides involvement in the design of curricula, businesses could also be more strongly involved in identifying graduate competencies for the assessment of programmes. Institutions should also be provided with enough human resource autonomy so that they can more flexibly redeploy academic staff according to those programmes which best respond to labour market needs (OECD, 2009a).

● *Fourth,* while some regions have started to introduce formula-based funding, partly based on performance indicators, funding of tertiary education institutions is still input-based in most regions, *i.e.* based on the number of students enrolled and the programmes provided. These are mostly decided in proposals put forward by the autonomous communities, and they do not react well to labour market demands (OECD, 2009a). Central and regional governments should move towards an output based funding of tertiary education, based on objective indicators – as was already recommended in earlier *OECD Economic Surveys* (OECD, 2008). This would also raise public spending efficiency beyond the effects on educational efficiency.

Helping the young to move from temporary to stable employment

Temporary contracts do not fulfil their role as a stepping stone to more regular jobs

Typically, employers tend to hire youth on temporary contracts whose productivity is not immediately observable. As a result, temporary employment may be a good entry path to the labour market, notably for youth who enter the labour market with adequate skills and get a chance to prove their productivity on relatively long temporary contracts (OECD, 2010a). However, Spain is unique in that temporary contracts are of very short duration and youth tend to stay on temporary contracts for a very long period of time (OECD, 2007). In Spain, almost 40% of less-educated and 20% of high-educated workers hold temporary contracts until the age of 39 (Figure 2.9). Moreover, positive and negative employment growth has been driven mainly by creation and cuts of temporary contracts with adverse effects in particular for young people (OECD, 2010b).

Figure 2.9. Young people are locked-in in temporary contracts

Temporary employment rates, by level of education, as a percentage of youth population per age group

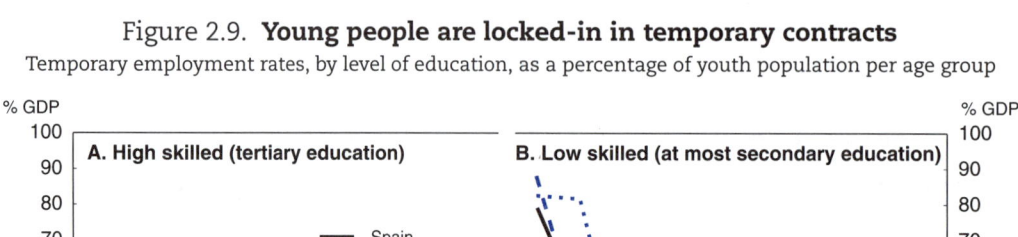
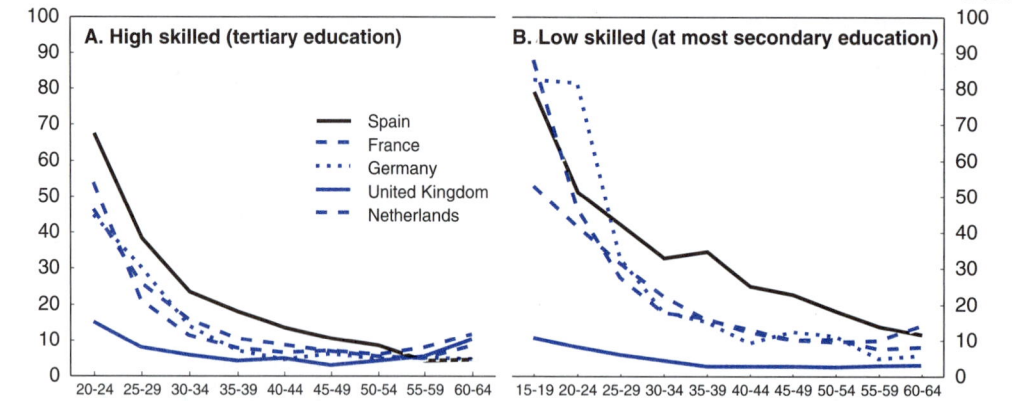

Source: Dolado *et al.* (2012), based on the yearly subsamples of the *European Labour Force Survey 2010*.

StatLink ⬛ *http://dx.doi.org/10.1787/888932740651*

One of the main reasons why temporary contracts do not act as a stepping stone in Spain is the large difference between dismissal costs for temporary contracts as compared to permanent ones which makes firms reluctant to transform temporary contracts into permanent ones. Even if firms are satisfied with the performance of the worker, it may still be cheaper to fire the worker and search for a new candidate, leading to excess turnover. Moreover, young people are trapped in precarious employment or unemployment, with adverse effects for their long-term employability and large costs for society as a whole. Two years after having been on a temporary contract, more than 22% of 15-29 year olds in Spain were still on temporary contracts, unemployed or inactive. In the United Kingdom, the number was less than 2% (OECD, 2010a).

Workers on temporary contracts are paid less than with permanent ones. Although, in principle, wage rates cannot be differentiated by contract type, researchers have found that in general, fixed-term workers earn somewhat less than comparable permanent employees, even if the wage differential falls when unobserved heterogeneity is accounted for. However, empirical estimates suggest that the wage penalty is higher in Spain than in other countries (Mertens et al., 2005). De la Rica (2004) estimates that, after controlling for heterogeneity in personal and job-related characteristics, permanent workers earn between 5 and 10% more than workers on temporary contracts. The evidence also indicates that the wage gap is associated with employers' decisions to under-classify temporary workers when assigning them to occupational categories (which determine their wage) (Bentolila et al., 2008).

Moreover, temporary contracts have adverse effects for economic growth (Mora-Sanguinetti and Fuentes, 2012). According to human capital theory, agents are more likely to invest in the acquisition of skills the longer is the post-training period over which they can amortise their investment. If either the firm or the worker expects job attachment to be short-term, then work-related training will either not be provided (the firm) or will not be accepted (the worker), depending on who bears the training costs (Arulampalam and Booth, 1998). Empirical evidence for Spain suggests that workers with temporary contracts are not only less likely to be employed in training firms but, once they are in those firms, they also have a lower probability of being chosen to participate in firm-provided training activities (Albert et al., 2005). Moreover, the prospect of starting on and remaining for some time on temporary contracts may reduce the effort exerted by workers on temporary contracts (Dolado and Stucchi, 2008) on top of their reduced incentives to invest in their own education (see also Mas-Ivars and Robledo-Domínguez, 2010).

The 2012 reform is a big step forward

The Spanish government has been introducing reforms of employment protection legislation since 2010, and equally in the 2012 labour market reform (Box 2.4).

The clearer definition of economic reasons has the potential to make it easier to have dismissal judged as justified, resulting in sharply lower severance payments of 20 days' wages per year of seniority (Box 2.4). Indeed, data suggest that the number of dismissals for objective reasons has already slightly increased recently from around 7% on average in 2010 to about 14% in the first quarter of 2012 (MLSS, 2012). The possibility to shed labour in bad times should raise the incentive of firms to use permanent contracts. Moreover, firms no longer have to pay interim wages while judicial procedures are pending and collective dismissals have been made easier by doing away with the requirement of approval by a regional or the central government. Hence, employees have less incentive to

Box 2.4. **The 2012 reform of employment protection legislation**

The 2012 labour market reforms aim to reduce further the duality in the Spanish labour market, with a reform of employment protection legislation and by fostering internal flexibility (see also Box 2.5):

- The law redefines the economic reasons for dismissal, further clarifying the conditions under which a dismissal for objective reasons could be justified. In this case, the employer pays 20 days' wages of severance pay per year of seniority. The law specifies that dismissal is justified for economic reasons if the company faces a persistent decline in revenues or income, *i.e.* over three consecutive quarters as compared to the same periods of the preceding year. As concerns other objective reasons for dismissal that would also justify justified dismissal, the firm has to show only that it has undertaken technical, organisational or other production process-related changes, but no longer has to prove that the dismissal was necessary for future profitability of the firm.

- If a dismissal is judged unjustified, the maximum severance pay is reduced to 33 days' wages per year of seniority up to a maximum of 24 months, compared with 45 days and a maximum of 42 months on the regular permanent contract before. This applies to all new contracts and for future years of service on existing contracts.

- The law eliminates the need for administrative authorisation of collective dismissal, in line with current regulations in most European countries.

- While it removes the option of express dismissal, according to which firms could declare the dismissal upfront as being "unjustified" and pay 45 days' wages per year of seniority to avoid litigation, firms no longer are obliged to pay interim wages during the period the case is adjudicated.

- The law introduces a new type of permanent contract for companies with fewer than 50 employees. Hiring on this new contract is subject to an extended trial period of one year, compared with a previous maximum of six months, and various tax credits (see Box 2.1).

- It further restricts the use of temporary contracts, by reinstating the maximum period of extension of a temporary contract to two years. This law was temporarily suspended in August 2011.

go to court *a priori*, to claim that the dismissal would have been unjustified. The reform has also removed the requirement that excessive unjustified absence from work could only justify dismissal of a worker if, at the same time, unjustified absence exceeded a threshold of 2.5% among the firm's employees on aggregate, which is welcome.

While the 2012 reform should facilitate restructuring and flexibility also in good times, it remains to be seen how many dismissals will be judged as justified by the courts then.[5] In any case and especially if most dismissals remain judged unjustified, severance pay for unjustified dismissal should be further reduced, as even at the current 33 days' wages per year of seniority, severance pay for unjustified dismissals remains high by international comparison. In particular, they would remain high in comparison with the dismissal costs on temporary contracts. Hence, if the reform does not prove effective in reducing duality substantially, introducing a single contract with initially low but increasing severance payments would reduce the difference in dismissal costs of temporary and permanent contracts more effectively. It would also hold the promise of a smoother transition from short to long-term employment.

The reform reinstates the pre-recession limit of 24 months on the duration of fixed-term contracts. While in theory this should improve incentives to hire permanent workers or convert temporary to permanent contracts, in practice it had little effect in the past. Moreover, it can be circumvented by firms through redefining the job and by rehiring workers on another temporary contract after an unemployment spell. In the medium term, introducing experience-rating of firms' contributions to the Unemployment insurance (UI) fund, as a complement to the introduction of a single contract proposed above, could reduce this incentive and eliminate this implicit subsidisation of temporary contracts. In such a system, employers' contributions to the unemployment insurance depend on the firm's dismissal history. At present, the government pays subsidies to small firms towards the cost of justified dismissals which amount to 40% of compensation in such cases. These subsidies are not an effective substitute for further reform of employment protection and may encourage excessive worker turnover at the expense of government finances. These subsidies should be abolished.

Improving firms' incentives for youth employment through more flexible collective bargaining

The collective bargaining system has had adverse effects on employment of young people

In Spain, firms have had limited leeway to adjust wages or working hours to economic conditions. This is due to a complex system of collective bargaining which takes place predominantly at the sectoral or regional level, and where bargaining outcomes are extended by law to all firms of the same sector or region, even if they are not represented in the agreement. Beyond the positive effects for overall employment and competitiveness as discussed above, making working conditions more flexible would be particularly helpful for hiring young people for the following reasons:

- Once firms are given more leeway in their wage setting, wages can again fulfil their role as price signal guiding workers and employers in their decision as concerns labour supply and demand, the matching of skills and jobs, or the investment in training or human capital accumulation (OECD, 2004).

- If firms cannot offer the median wage to new employees, which may be the case especially for smaller firms, they can attract young qualified people by making other working conditions more interesting. For instance, firms could more easily hire on part-time jobs, which would be attractive for those young people who want to continue with higher-level education or training. Part-time jobs would also make it easier for women with children to stay in work, which would have a double dividend as it would raise female participation in the labour force and increase potential growth. In the past, part-time work was relatively rare in Spain as compared to other countries (Figure 2.10), which was mainly linked to the rigid collective bargaining system where firms did not have much leeway in setting or changing working hours.

- Well functioning collective bargaining is not only an important factor for job creation in itself, but it is also a fundamental complement to other reforms, especially of employment protection described above. More flexible collective bargaining on the firm level would give firms an alternative to dismissing workers if things turn sour, hence would hire more easily on permanent contracts *a priori*. This could also make the subsidies for hiring on permanent contracts, including the new permanent contract for small enterprises, redundant (see above).

Figure 2.10. **The use of part-time work is not very frequent**

Percentage share of part-time employment in total dependent employment by sex, 15-24 year-olds, 2011

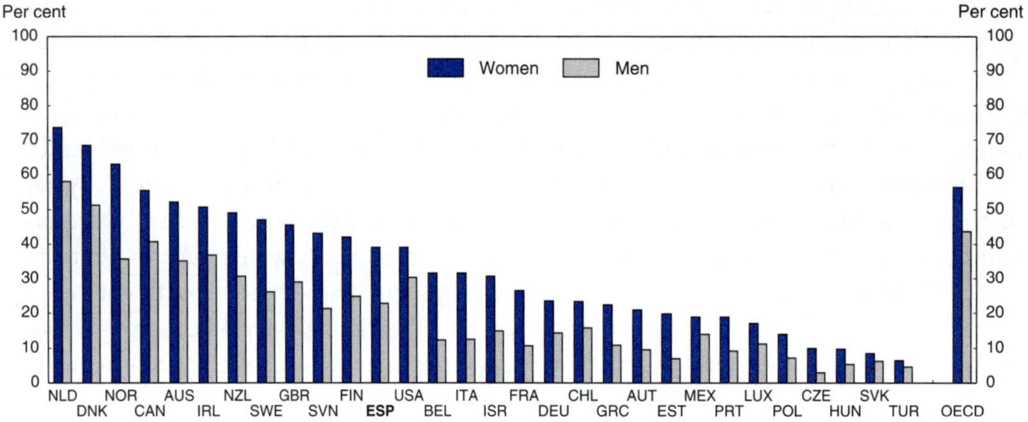

Source: OECD (2012), *Labour Force Statistics Database*, November.

StatLink ⬛ᴵᶩ http://dx.doi.org/10.1787/888932740670

The 2012 reform should help

The government has been introducing reforms of the collective bargaining system since 2010, and also most recently in 2012 (Box 2.5). The 2012 labour market reform allows companies to reach firm-level collective agreements, removing the restrictions that sector-level bargaining could impose on such agreements. Firms can more easily opt-out from collective agreements, even if employers and workers fail to agree; in this case, binding arbitration procedures apply. Moreover, firms can unilaterally alter employment contracts. Finally, the reform limits to one year the maximum time period during which the conditions of a collective agreement remain in force beyond the period originally foreseen in the agreement.

These steps significantly improve flexibility of work conditions at the firm level which is welcome. Recent data show wage moderation is taking place: wage increases agreed in collective bargaining diminished in September to 1.3% and even further 0.3% in the case of new agreements. Nevertheless, shortcomings remain. The limit of automatic extension provides social partners a stronger incentive to respond to changes in economic conditions, lowering to some extent the relevance of the legal extension. However, some collective wage agreements may still apply for up to 4 years as some are negotiated for 3 years and could be in force for another year following the originally foreseen end period. This could make wages less responsive to economic conditions, although the measures described above improve flexibility and nominal year-on-year wage growth per worker fell to 0% in the second quarter 2012. For firms failing to reach a firm-level agreement, legal extension requires them to apply higher-level agreements.

High-level agreements may become more flexible to changes in economic conditions in response to the implemented reforms. Still, the outcomes of new firm-level agreements are likely to remain conditioned by legally extended sectoral agreements, as these will in most cases provide the fall-back option if a firm-level agreement is not reached. Another option to address these shortcomings could be to abolish the legal extension principle and replacing it with an opt-in system where employers decide *ex ante* whether to be represented in sectoral wage bargaining.

> ### Box 2.5. **The 2012 reform of collective bargaining**
>
> One of the main building blocks of the 2012 labour market reforms concerns the collective bargaining system so as to enhance adaptability of firms to shocks. It also aims at reducing labour market duality by fostering the internal flexibility of firms:
>
> - It allows companies to reach a collective agreement with representatives of workers to establish relevant working conditions within the firm, most notably including basic salary, allowances and overtime compensation, or the distribution of working time. These firm-level agreements have priority vis-à-vis higher-level agreements.
>
> - If there is no collective agreement on the firm-level, the new law aims to further facilitate opting out from higher level agreements. No further condition applies to opt-out as concerns working hours, wages, work location or functions, if the firm has suffered declining revenues for two consecutive quarters as compared to the same periods of the preceding year. Opting out is also easier to justify for technical, organisational or production-related reasons. In particular, the law introduces obligatory arbitration if workers and employers do not agree on the conditions of the opt-out.
>
> - If a firm suffers declining revenues over two consecutive quarters, it can unilaterally alter or suspend employment contracts beyond what was originally agreed between employers and workers. Changing a contract unilaterally by the employer is possible under economic, technical, organisational or production-related reasons – similar to dismissal for justified reasons (see above Box 2.4) and opting out. In case of disagreement with the decision of the employer, the employee may choose to charge compensation of 20 days per year worked and terminate the employment relationship or appeal before the Social Courts.
>
> - The reform aims to encourage more flexible renegotiation of the agreements and reduce their inertia. It sets a maximum of one year (ultra-actividad) during which a former agreement is valid. If there was no new agreement within this one year, labor relations would be governed by the provisions of the agreement at higher levels. This would be a sectoral or regional agreement, or if also this is not renewed, the Workers' Statute.

An opting-in system would in particular be preferable to the option under the new law for firms to unilaterally alter or even suspend employment contracts, under certain conditions, beyond what was originally agreed between employers and workers. The prospect of such *ex post* changes of working contracts may create uncertainty among workers – despite the existence of a court ruling that aims to increase legal certainty in the application of internal flexibility measures. Unnecessary uncertainty may also be introduced by new provisions which make it easier for firms to fire workers if they have been absent from the workplace, including in cases in which such absence is justified (*e.g.* illness which is not work-related and of a duration of less than 20 days). For example, a justified absence of 9 days within a 2 month-period is a valid cause for justified dismissal. In the short-term, both types of uncertainty may harm consumer confidence, potentially resulting in a loss of activity. In the medium term, these rules may encourage inefficient human resource management within the firm, with perhaps adverse effects on productivity.

Box 2.6. **Recommendations on improving employment prospects for young workers**

Ensuring that youth-at-risk remain connected to the labour market

- Post-recession, abolish subsidies for hiring the unemployed on permanent contracts, and in any case, target them solely on the most disadvantaged or difficult to place youth.

- Provide the most disadvantaged youth access to closely monitored job-search assistance programmes and increase training measures.

Reinforcing the mutual obligation system of unemployment insurance

- Introduce comprehensive monitoring and evaluation of placement services and ALMP implementation at regional level based on quantitative output indicators.

- Start entitlement to unemployment benefits at registration and do not pay benefits retroactively from registration. Make the first intensive interview mandatory at the time of registration and increase the frequency of placement interviews. Reinforce the requirement for unemployed to take on a suitable job.

- In the longer term, the government may consider reducing the duration of unemployment benefits.

Reducing the early drop-out rate from education

- Narrow the criteria for granting pupils promotion to subsequent grades to those core competencies that are needed to follow any type of upper secondary education.

- Introduce loans with income-contingent repayments for tertiary education and improve access to grants for students from socially disadvantaged families.

Improving upper secondary vocational education

- Combine school-based vocational education and training contracts within a single scheme, extend the period for which training contracts are signed, and provide work-based training through training contracts alternated with school-based training.

- Involve firms more strongly in the curriculum of school-based training and open up the teaching profession in vocational schools more widely to practitioners.

Ensuring that tertiary education graduates leave with skills demanded by the labour market

- Involve business actors more widely in bodies providing advice to educational policy authorities and in the governing councils of tertiary education institutions. Involve businesses also more strongly in identifying graduate competencies for the assessment of study programmes.

- Ensure that institutions have enough human resource autonomy so that they can more flexibly redeploy academic staff according to those programmes which best respond to labour market needs.

- Integrate higher vocational education into the tertiary education system.

- Central and regional governments should move towards an output based funding of tertiary education, based on objective indicators.

Box 2.6. **Recommendations on improving employment prospects for young workers** *(cont.)*

Helping the young to move from temporary to stable employment

- Further reduce severance pay for unjustified dismissal. If the reform does not prove effective in reducing duality substantially, a single contract with initially low but gradually increasing severance payments would help reduce the still large difference in dismissal costs between temporary and permanent contracts.

- Reduce the 1-year probationary period for small enterprises in line with other contracts.

- The subsidies to small firms towards their cost of justified dismissals should be abolished.

Improving firms' incentives for youth employment through more flexible collective bargaining

- An option to improve the flexibility to react to economic conditions is to abolish legal extension of higher level collective bargaining agreements or replace it by an opt-in system, where employers decide whether to be represented in sectoral wage bargaining.

Notes

1. Unemployed older than 24 years or with dependent children, whose unemployment benefits have been exhausted, have access to social assistance. The maximum amount of social assistance is about 18% of the average wage, with differences in the rate across regions. Furthermore, unemployed older than 45 years have access to unemployment assistance (OECD, 2011d).

2. These estimates are based on the assumption that students who repeat grades attain, at most, lower secondary education. If they were to attain higher levels of education, the costs would be even greater.

3. This assumes that students self-select into general *versus* vocational upper secondary education based on their perceived capabilities (Wolter and Ryan, 2011).

4. *Contratos de formación (CF)* are contracts targeted at youth aged 16-21 with an upper secondary education degree and for individuals belonging to specific target groups for training in a firm. They last at least six months but no more than two years. Employers receive a subsidy to cover training costs and accident insurance for the students. As a counterpart, employers have the obligation of providing training of at least 15% of the time spent in the firm to be dedicated to training. At the end of the contract period, employers have to issue a certificate containing information on the duration of the contract, job content and major assignments carried out by the trainee. Trainees are paid a salary set in collective agreements within the limits established by law and which cannot be lower than the minimum wage (OECD, 2007).

5. There are also some issues with interpretation of the new rule. For instance, a firm that had a 1% fall in revenue for three consecutive quarters would be able to dismiss workers while a firm that suffered a 30% fall in revenue for two consecutive quarters could not.

Bibliography

Albert, C., C. Garcia-Serrano and V. Hernanz (2005), "Firm-provided training and temporary contracts", *Spanish Economic Review*, No. 7, pp. 67-88.

Arellano, M., S. Bentolila and O. Bover (1998), "Unemployment Duration, Benefit Duration and the Business Cycle", *CEPR Discussion Paper*, No. 1840, Centre for Economic Policy Research, London.

Arulampalam, W. and A.L. Booth (1998), "Training and Labour Market Flexibility: Is There a Trade-off?", *British Journal of Industrial Relations 1998*, No. 36, pp. 521-536.

Bentolila, S., J.J. Dolado and J.F. Jimeno (2008), "Two-Tier Employment Protection Reforms: The Spanish Experience", *CESifo DICE Report*, Vol. 6, No. 4, CESifo Group, Munich.

Bundesagentur für Arbeit (BfA) (2012), "Ausbildung von A bis Z", Nürnberg.

De la Rica, S. (2004), "Wage Gaps between Workers with Indefinite and Fixed-Term Contracts: The Impact of Firm and Occupational Segregation", *Moneda y Crédito*, No. 219, pp. 43-69.

De Serres, A., F. Murtin, C. de la Maisonneuve (2012), "Tackling Unemployment in a Weak Post-Crisis Recovery: Policies to Facilitate the Return to Work", forthcoming as *OECD Economics Department Working Papers*, OECD Publishing.

Dolado, J.J. and R.M. Stucchi (2008), "Do Temporary Contracts Affect TFP? Evidence from Spanish Manufacturing Firms", *IZA Discussion Papers*, No. 3832.

Dolado, J.J., F. Felgueroso, M. Jensen, A. Fuentes and A. Wölfl (2012), "The Youth Labour Market in Spain", forthcoming as *OECD Economics Department Working Papers*, OECD, Paris.

Education, Audiovisual and Culture Executive Agency (Eurydice) (2012), "The European Higher Education Area in 2012", *Bologna Process Implementation Report*, Brussels.

El Pais (2012), "El PP endurece la reforma laboral al acortar la prórroga de los convenios", *http://economia.elpais.com/economia/2012/05/24/actualidad/1337853481_327630.html*.

Felgueroso, F., M. Hidalgo and S. Jiménez-Martin (2010), "Explaining the Fall of the Skill Wage Premium in Spain", *Fedea Working Paper*, Madrid.

García-Pérez, J.I., M. Hidalgo-Hidalgo and J.A. Robles-Zurita (2011), "Does Grade Retention Affect Achievement?", some evidence from PISA, *University Pablo de Olavide Working Paper*, Sevilla.

Höckel, K. (2008), *Costs and Benefits in Vocational Education and Training*, OECD Publishing.

Krause, M.U. and T.A. Lubik (2007), "On-the-Job-Search and the Cyclical Dynamics of the Labour Market", *ECB Working Paper*, No. 779, July 2007, Frankfurt.

Kuczera, M., G. Brunello, S. Field and N. Hoffman (2008), "A Learning for Jobs Review of Norway", OECD Publishing.

Martin, J.P. and D. Grubb (2001), "What Works and for Whom: A Review of OECD Countries' Experiences with Active Labour Market Policies", *Swedish Economic Policy Review*, Vol. 8, No. 2.

Mas-Ivars, M. and J.C. Robledo Domínguez (2010), "Productividad. Una perspectiva internacional y sectorial, Fundación BBVA", Madrid.

Mertens, A., V. Gash and F. McGinnity (2005), "The Cost of Flexibility at the Margin. Comparing the Wage Penalty for Fixed-Term Contracts in Germany and Spain using Quantile Regression".

Ministerio de Educación, de Cultura y Deporte (MECD) (2012), *www.educacion.gob.es/educacion/que-estudiar-y-donde/educacion-secundaria-obligatoria.html*.

Ministerio de Empleo y Seguridad Social (MESS) (2012), *Bulletin of Labour Market Statistics*.

Ministerio de Trabajo y Immigración (MTI) (2008), "Overview of the Vocational Education and Training System – Spain".

Mohrenweiser, J. and T. Zwick (2009), "Why do firms train apprentices? The net cost puzzle reconsidered", in *Labour Economics*, No. 16, pp. 631-637, Elsevier.

Mora-Sanguinetti, J.S. and A. Fuentes (2012), "An Analysis of Productivity Performance in Spain Before and During the Crisis: Exploring the Role of Institutions", *OECD Economics Department Working Papers*, No. 973, OECD Publishing.

Muehlemann, S., H. Pfeifer, G. Walden, F. Wenzelmann and S.C. Wolter (2010), "The Financing of Apprenticeship Training in the Light of Labour Market Regulations", in *Labour Economics*, No. 17, pp. 799-809.

National Institute for Statistics (INE) (2012), *Labour Force Statistics*.

OECD (2004), "Wage-setting Institutions and Outcomes", Chapter 3 of 2004, *OECD Employment Outlook*, OECD Publishing.

OECD (2006), *OECD Employment Outlook 2006*, OECD Publishing.

OECD (2007), *Jobs for Youth: Spain*, OECD Publishing.

OECD (2008), *OECD Economic Surveys: Spain*, OECD Publishing.

OECD (2009a), *OECD Reviews of Tertiary Education*, OECD Publishing.

OECD (2009b), "How do Industry, Firm and Worker Characteristics Shape Job and Worker Flows?", Chapter 2 in *OECD Employment Outlook 2009*, OECD Publishing.

OECD (2010a), *Off to a Good Start, Jobs for Youth*, OECD Publishing.

OECD (2010b), *OECD Economic Surveys: Spain*, OECD Publishing.

OECD (2010c), *OECD Employment Outlook*, OECD Publishing.

OECD (2010d), *Learning for the Job – OECD Reviews of Vocational Education and Training*, OECD Publishing.

OECD (2011a), *Pisa in Focus 2011/6*, OECD Publishing.

OECD (2011b), *Education at a Glance*, OECD Publishing.

OECD (2011c), "Right for the Job: Over-qualified or Under-skilled?", Chapter 4 in *OECD Employment Outlook*, OECD Publishing.

OECD (2011d), *Benefits and Wages: Spain 2010*, OECD Publishing.

OECD (2012a), *Equity and Quality in Education: Supporting Disadvantaged Students and Schools*, OECD Publishing.

OECD (2012b), *OECD Reviews of Vocational Education and Training: A Commentary on Spain*, forthcoming.

OECD (2012c), *Education at a Glance*, OECD Publishing.

Scarpetta, S., A. Sonnet and T. Manfredi (2010), "Rising Youth Unemployment During the Crisis: How to Prevent Negative Long-term Consequences on a Generation?", *OECD Social, Employment and Migration Working Papers*, No. 106, OECD, Paris.

Wolter, S.C. and P. Ryan (2011), "Apprenticeship", in *Handbook of the Economics of Education*, Vol. 3, Elsevier.

ORGANISATION FOR ECONOMIC CO-OPERATION AND DEVELOPMENT

The OECD is a unique forum where governments work together to address the economic, social and environmental challenges of globalisation. The OECD is also at the forefront of efforts to understand and to help governments respond to new developments and concerns, such as corporate governance, the information economy and the challenges of an ageing population. The Organisation provides a setting where governments can compare policy experiences, seek answers to common problems, identify good practice and work to co-ordinate domestic and international policies.

The OECD member countries are: Australia, Austria, Belgium, Canada, Chile, the Czech Republic, Denmark, Estonia, Finland, France, Germany, Greece, Hungary, Iceland, Ireland, Israel, Italy, Japan, Korea, Luxembourg, Mexico, the Netherlands, New Zealand, Norway, Poland, Portugal, the Slovak Republic, Slovenia, Spain, Sweden, Switzerland, Turkey, the United Kingdom and the United States. The European Union takes part in the work of the OECD.

OECD Publishing disseminates widely the results of the Organisation's statistics gathering and research on economic, social and environmental issues, as well as the conventions, guidelines and standards agreed by its members.

OECD PUBLISHING, 2, rue André-Pascal, 75775 PARIS CEDEX 16
(10 2012 18 1 P) ISBN 978-92-64-412832-3 – No. 60327 2012-02